Searching for Heaven *on* Earth

How to Find What Really Matters in Life

Ecclesiastes 1:1–12:12

DR. DAVID JEREMIAH

P.O. Box 3838
San Diego, CA 92163

Unless otherwise indicated, Scripture verses quoted are taken from the NEW KING JAMES VERSION.

Printed in the United States of America.

CONTENTS

About Dr. David Jeremiah and Turning Point . . 4

About This Study Guide 5

Introduction. 7

1. The Futility of Life
Ecclesiastes 1:1–11 9

2. Sorting Out Your Life
Ecclesiastes 1:12–2:26 17

3. Beautiful in His Time
Ecclesiastes 3:1–15 27

4. When Your World Doesn't Make Sense
Ecclesiastes 3:16–4:16 37

5. Taking Your Troubles to Church
Ecclesiastes 5:1–20 47

6. The Cul-de-Sacs of Life
Ecclesiastes 6:1–12 57

7. When Bad Is Better
Ecclesiastes 7:1–10 67

8. Wisdom to Be Thankful For
Ecclesiastes 7:11–29 77

9. Facing Life With Humility
Ecclesiastes 8:1–17 87

10. The Subject Nobody Talks About
Ecclesiastes 9:1–18 97

11. Fools Rush In
Ecclesiastes 10:1–20 107

12. Before It's Too Late
Ecclesiastes 11:1–12:14. 117

Resources 126

Contact Information. 128

About Dr. David Jeremiah and Turning Point

Dr. David Jeremiah is the founder of Turning Point, a ministry committed to providing Christians with sound Bible teaching relevant to today's changing times through radio and television broadcasts, audio series, books, and live events. Dr. Jeremiah's common-sense teaching on topics such as family, prayer, worship, angels, and biblical prophecy forms the foundation of Turning Point.

David and his wife, Donna, reside in El Cajon, California, where he serves as the senior pastor of Shadow Mountain Community Church. David and Donna have four children and eleven grandchildren.

In 1982, Dr. Jeremiah brought the same solid teaching to San Diego television that he shares weekly with his congregation. Shortly thereafter, Turning Point expanded its ministry to radio.Dr. Jeremiah's inspiring messages can now be heard worldwide on radio, television, and the Internet.

Because Dr. Jeremiah desires to know his listening audience, he travels nationwide holding ministry rallies and spiritual enrichment conferences that touch the hearts and lives of many people. According to Dr. Jeremiah, "At some point in time, everyone reaches a turning point; and for every person, that moment is unique, an experience to hold onto forever. There's so much changing in today's world that sometimes it's difficult to choose the right path. Turning Point offers people an understanding of God's Word as well as the opportunity to make a difference in their lives."

Dr. Jeremiah has authored numerous books, including ***Escape the Coming Night*** (Revelation)*,* ***The Handwriting on the Wall*** (Daniel)*,* ***Overcoming Loneliness, Grand Parenting, The Joy of Encouragement, Prayer—The Great Adventure, God in You*** (Holy Spirit)*,* ***Gifts from God*** (Parenting)*,* ***Jesus' Final Warning, When Your World Falls Apart, Slaying the Giants in Your Life, My Heart's Desire, Sanctuary, Searching for Heaven on Earth, The Secret of the Light, Captured by Grace, Discover Paradise, Grace Givers, Why the Nativity?, Signs of Life, What in the World Is Going On?, The Coming Economic Armageddon, I Never Thought I'd See the Day!, and God Loves You: He Always Has—He Always Will.***

About This Study Guide

The purpose of this Turning Point study guide is to reinforce Dr. David Jeremiah's dynamic, in-depth teaching and to aid the reader in applying biblical truth to his or her daily life. This study guide is designed to be used in conjunction with Dr. Jeremiah's ***Searching for Heaven on Earth*** audio series, but it may also be used by itself for personal or group study.

Structure of the Lessons

Each lesson is based on one of the messages in the ***Searching for Heaven on Earth*** compact disc series and focuses on specific passages in the Bible. Each lesson is composed of the following elements:

- *Outline*

The outline at the beginning of the lesson gives a clear, concise picture of the topic being studied and provides a helpful framework for readers as they listen to Dr. Jeremiah's teaching.

- *Overview*

The overview summarizes Dr. Jeremiah's teaching on the passage being studied in the lesson. Readers should refer to the Scripture passages in their own Bibles as they study the overview. Unless otherwise indicated, Scripture verses quoted are taken from the New King James Version.

- *Application*

This section contains a variety of questions designed to help readers dig deeper into the lesson and the Scriptures, and to apply the lesson to their daily lives. For Bible study groups or Sunday school classes, these questions will provide a springboard for group discussion and interaction.

- *Did You Know?*

This section presents a fascinating fact, historical note, or insight that adds a point of interest to the preceding lesson.

Using This Guide for Group Study

The lessons in this study guide are suitable for Sunday school classes, small-group studies, elective Bible studies, or home Bible study groups. Each person in the group should have his or her own study guide.

When possible, the study guide should be used with the corresponding compact disc series. You may wish to assign the study guide lesson as homework prior to the meeting of the group and then use the meeting time to listen to the CD and discuss the lesson.

For Continuing Study

For a complete listing of Dr. Jeremiah's materials for personal and group study call 1-800-947-1993, go online to www.DavidJeremiah.org, or write to: Turning Point, P.O. Box 3838, San Diego, CA 92163.

Dr. Jeremiah's ***Turning Point*** program is currently heard or viewed around the world on radio, television, and the Internet in English. ***Momento Decisivo,*** the Spanish translation of Dr. Jeremiah's messages, can be heard on radio in every Spanish speaking country in the world. The television broadcast is also broadcast by satellite throughout the Middle East with Arabic subtitles.

Contact Turning Point for radio and television program times and stations in your area. Or visit our website at www.DavidJeremiah.org.

SEARCHING FOR HEAVEN ON EARTH

INTRODUCTION

One of the most amazing stories in the Old Testament concerns an obscure city called Abel (2 Samuel 20). This city had a reputation in Israel as being filled with wise people. The example we have of Abel's wisdom is startling.

David had given orders to his men to do away with a trouble-maker named Sheba. So Joab, the commander of David's men, set out to find and kill Sheba. Sheba took refuge in Abel, hoping the city would protect him. When the city's residents saw that Joab was prepared to destroy the city in order to get to Sheba, a "wise woman" called out to him. She asked Joab why he was going to destroy Abel and this "mother in Israel." Joab said all he wanted was Sheba—he would spare the city if they would deliver the fugitive to him.

The woman told Joab (in essence), "Wait right there." Shortly, the head of Sheba came sailing over the city wall! Joab packed up his troops and returned to Jerusalem—mission accomplished.

Did the residents of Abel live up to their reputation for wisdom? In the purest sense of the Hebrew word for wisdom, they absolutely did. Wisdom meant "skill" in the Old Testament, and the residents of Abel were filled with it. They weighed their options—protect Sheba or protect themselves—and chose the latter.

In our genteel day, we might be a little shocked at that display of wisdom. We think of a wise person as someone who is quiet, thoughtful, and studious, dispensing wisdom in clipped phrases from the comfort of a wing-backed chair. But in the Old Testament, wisdom was a matter of observation and implementation.

The wisest man in the Old Testament was Solomon, and he wrote the book of Ecclesiastes (and Proverbs and Song of Solomon as well). Solomon demonstrated Abel-like tendencies himself (1 Kings 3:16–28). The book of Ecclesiastes displays Solomon's observation-implementation skill applied to evaluating life itself. It was written after Solomon spent many years observing what worked and what didn't work about life. He had wandered away from the God of his youth, the wife of his youth, and the worldview of his youth, and found himself a discouraged and regretful old king.

For decades, Solomon tried to find meaning in life through riches, extravagant and profligate living, his work as king, and through the study of philosophies and beliefs of others. Ecclesiastes is the history of that ill-fated search, written at the end of his life when he came back to the conclusion of his youth: God is at the center of life and to ignore Him makes life vain and meaningless. Life is a matter of deceptive illusions when it is lived apart from God.

It's a shame that Solomon's great skill had to be applied in a search to which he already possessed the answer. God had given Solomon his wisdom as a young king; he knew there was no life apart from God (1 Kings 3:4–15). But he spent years proving what he had learned in his youth—and then wrote a book full of his observations.

In the end, Solomon got it right. Like the residents of Abel, he weighed his options and chose correctly. His "conclusion of the whole matter" is that "man's all" is to "fear God and keep His commandments" (12:13). Almost too late, he validated his own reputation as the wisest man in Israel.

Fortunately, God has given us Ecclesiastes to spare us our own search for the meaning of life. Observe Solomon's search and implement his solution. It's the wisest thing you could possibly do.

THE FUTILITY OF LIFE

Ecclesiastes 1:1–11

In this lesson we are introduced to the theme of Ecclesiastes.

OUTLINE

Many people today are searching for meaning in life, but in all the wrong places. Trying to find eternal meaning in a temporal world is like trying to fit a square peg into a round hole. God made us for eternity, and only His eternal presence in our lives can satisfy our thirst for meaning.

I. The Futility of Life
   A. The Course of Life
   B. The Circle of the Sun
   C. The Circuit of the Winds
   D. The Cycle of Water

II. The Frustration of Life
   A. Nothing Is Fulfilling
   B. Nothing Is Fresh

OVERVIEW

When social scientists from Johns Hopkins University surveyed nearly 8,000 students at 48 different colleges on what issues they considered most important in their lives, 16 percent said "making a lot of money" was their goal. But 75 percent said their primary goal was to find meaning and purpose in life.

Pastor Rick Warren's book, *The Purpose-Driven Life,* became a best seller because it focused on the need for every person to discover his or her purpose in life. In his book, Warren notes a survey conducted by Dr. Hugh Moorhead in which he wrote to 250 leading intellectuals and scientists asking them, "What is the meaning of life?" Most had little to offer in terms of a philosophy. In fact, some wrote Moorhead and said, "If you find out what the purpose of life is, please let me know."

A college student wrote this note before taking his own life: "To anyone in the world who cares, Who am I? Why am I living? Life has become stupid and purposeless. Nothing makes sense to me anymore. The questions I had when I came to college are still unanswered and now I am convinced there are no answers. There can only be pain and guilt and despair here in this world. My fear of death and the unknown is far less terrifying than the prospect of the unbearable frustration, futility, and hopelessness of continued existence."

The search for meaning and purpose in life is the most profound study upon which one can embark. And the book of Ecclesiastes, written by Solomon, chronicles his own search to find the purpose of life. It is unique in the Bible as it tells of a man's philosophical search for meaning and describes the conclusions he reached.

Solomon wrote three books: Song of Solomon as a young man; Proverbs as a middle-aged man, and Ecclesiastes in his latter years—his book of regrets. He looked back over his life and realized how many foolish choices he made in his search to find the meaning of life. Fortunately, he came to a godly conclusion at the end of the book, but it was too late for him to enjoy it personally.

Solomon was in a unique position to conduct a study on the meaning of life. His 40-year reign as king of Israel was a time of peace, so he was not occupied with wars. He had plenty of money and resources that allowed him to undertake a study. And he had the mental capacity to consider weighty matters: He was the wisest, smartest man of his age, perhaps of all time (1:16).

The word "Ecclesiastes" means "the gathering." Solomon calls himself, in Hebrew, *qohelet*, or "the preacher" or "the quester." He was a man on a mission—a mission to discover the meaning of life.

Are you one of those people (like my dear wife) who will turn to the last chapter of a novel and read it first in order to learn the conclusion of the matter? Solomon saves you the trouble in Ecclesiastes. He states his conclusion right up front: "Vanity of vanities . . . all is vanity" (1:2). The word "vanity" is used 38 times in Ecclesiastes. That qualifies it as a primary theme of the author. But it is not the vanity of beauty or vainglory we are familiar with today.

Instead, he means that life is something that doesn't work—it is a vain pursuit to try to find ultimate meaning in this life alone. Life is a vapor that is not permanent, Solomon concluded after his investigation. It will not bear the weighty title of Meaningful and Purposeful. "Vanity of vanities" is a Hebraism—a way in Solomon's language to express intensity. He was dead serious about the fact that the search for meaning in life alone is a vain pursuit. Because life is empty, Solomon asks, "What's there to show for a lifetime of work, a lifetime of working your fingers to the bone?" (1:3, *The Message*).

Many have misunderstood Solomon's questions and answers. Here is the key to understanding the book: Solomon is describing life as if there is no God at all in the picture. And his conclusion is that life is meaningless without Him. His phrase "under the sun" (used 29 times in the book) is how he expresses his description of life in terms of the world without God. In this sense, Solomon is like many people today—trying to find meaning in life without God. In this book, Solomon will conclude that life has no meaning apart from God.

The Futility of Life (1:4-7)

Solomon begins by teaching us four things about the futility of life.

The Course of Life (1:4)

"One generation passes . . . and another generation comes" (verse 4). Solomon might have been reading one of our modern, small-town newspapers that records the births and deaths in the community on a daily basis. The same day a baby is born, an elderly person dies. Generations come and generations go. Man is transient, but the earth stays the same. Solomon is thinking about these issues as he nears the end of his own life.

In one of his books, Rabbi Harold Kushner recounts what a man told him in a conversation:

"Two weeks ago, for the first time in my life, I went to the funeral of a man my own age. I didn't know him well, but we worked together, talked to each other from time to time, had kids about the same age. He died suddenly over the weekend. A bunch of us went to the funeral, each of us thinking, 'It could just as easily have been me.' That was two weeks ago. They have already replaced him at the office. I hear his wife is moving out of state to live with her parents. Two weeks ago, he was working fifty feet away from me; and now it's as if he never existed. It's like a rock falling into a pool of water, and then the water is the same as it was before, but the rock isn't there anymore. Rabbi, I've hardly slept at all since then. I can't stop thinking that it could happen to me, and a few days later I will be forgotten as if I had never lived. Shouldn't a man's life be more than that?"

Many people are asking similar questions today. Isn't there more to life than the same daily cycle of work-sleep-work-sleep, followed by death? Solomon is saying that, from that perspective, life seems futile and meaningless. And it is hard to disagree with him.

The Circle of the Sun (1:5)

Solomon says the cycle of meaninglessness is illustrated by the sun: "The sun also rises, and the sun goes down, and hastens to the place where it arose" (verse 5). Modern astronomers talk about the sun rising and setting just as Solomon did. It's a figure of speech today since we know the sun doesn't "rise" and "set," but Solomon thought it moved across the sky in a repetitive cycle that was endless. Or meaningless, to be more precise. Rise, set, rise, set—every day the same thing.

The Circuit of the Winds (1:6)

The wind is also a natural phenomenon that seems to follow endless paths in the sky: "The wind whirls about continually, and comes again on its circuit" (verse 6). It is amazing that Solomon could make these observations about nature long before the modern scientific era with its analytical tools. We are used to seeing the satellite image maps that TV weathermen use to show the jet stream and its effects. But Solomon simply observed the cycles of nature in his search for meaning and concluded that even nature was repetitive and meaningless.

The Cycle of Water (1:7)

Water is a great example of repetitiveness. "The rivers run into the sea," which never gets full. How does this happen? Solomon didn't know about evaporation that creates clouds that create rain that fills the rivers that run into the sea. But he saw a cycle which seemed just as meaningless as life.

The wind, the sun, the water—they're all like life. They come and they go, repeating themselves over and over. There is a mechanical monotony to the way the world turns, a seeming futility when you consider it apart from God.

Have you ever thought these thoughts? It's easy even for Christians to get caught up in the morose thinking of a world that seems pointless. We begin to wonder, Why am I here? When we fail to remember God, we can find ourselves as despondent as Solomon did.

THE FRUSTRATION OF LIFE (1:8–11)

From the frustration of life, Solomon moves to the futility of life.

Nothing Is Fulfilling (1:8)

We could easily translate verse eight as, "Life is B-O-R-I-N-G!" There is a restlessness in the human heart apart from God, a restlessness born out of a failure to find meaning. We are always looking for something new, something better, the next thing to fill the void we feel if we don't know God.

Isn't that what the entertainment industry is all about? And the devolution of that industry, where promoters and media executives are in a continual search for the next bizarre television show or form of entertainment that will occupy our bored and restless hearts? A person who doesn't have God in his life is focused on the lives of others—the stars, the wealthy, the interesting. We try to relieve our boredom by looking into the lives of others who, if truth be told, are as bored as everyone else—if they don't know God.

In Acts 17 we have the record of the apostle Paul's encounter with the Athenians who spent their time talking about what's new. Novelty . . . the latest and greatest . . . that's what they were all about. J. Vernon McGee used to say, "If it's new, it's not true; and if it's true, it's not new." And he was right.

The constant desire to acquire newer, better, bigger, and faster "things" is another evidence of our insatiable restlessness. Computers, televisions, electronic gadgets, cars, houses—even marriage partners—the constant quest for greener grass on the other side of the fence is an evidence of our restless hearts, living life apart from God. Nothing can fulfill a heart that is centered only in this world.

Nothing Is Fresh (1:9–11)

Not only is nothing fulfilling, nothing is fresh. Everything seems stale, something we've seen or done before. And it's true, for there is nothing new under the sun.

That may not resonate with you. There are new inventions, new products, new discoveries, new adventures. What Solomon means is that nothing new is being created by God. What God created in the beginning is all that has ever been created. Anything we invent is just a rearrangement of something God already created. Thomas Edison once said that his inventions were only applying the secrets of nature for the happiness of mankind. He created nothing new, for there is nothing new under the sun.

Solomon's message in this book is going to be that nothing in this world can fulfill or satisfy the longings of the human soul except God. Solomon knows this because at one time in his life He was close to God; he knew the fulfillment that God can bring. He prayed and God granted him a heart of wisdom. But he allowed his heart to be led away from God by his great wealth, wisdom, and women so that he died, I believe, a disillusioned and discouraged old man.

Solomon had once been connected to heaven, but he forsook the God of his youth and gradually lost the meaning of life. And he came to realize, expressed in Ecclesiastes, that life has no meaning apart from God. His decades-long search for fulfillment ended in frustration: "For who knows what is good for man in life, all the days of his vain life which he passes like a shadow?" (6:12)

One of the keys to this book is found in 3:11: "He has put eternity in their hearts." The heart of man is oriented toward eternity, and there is nothing in this temporal world that can satisfy it. If we try to fill the eternity-shaped void in our heart with something temporal, it's like trying to fit a square peg in a round hole. It won't fit and we walk away frustrated and confused.

The only way to experience the eternity that God put in your heart is to allow the eternal God to take up residence in your heart through Jesus Christ. It was this Jesus who said, "I have come that they may have life, and that they may have it more abundantly" (John 10:10b). Only Jesus can give you the life you were created to enjoy.

APPLICATION

1. Read Psalm 73.

   a. What does the metaphor in verse 2 suggest?

   Almost lost the sight of God

   b. How does the psalmist summarize what almost caused him to stumble? (verse 3)

   Envy

   c. Explain verses 2–3 in terms of the meaning of life. How did the psalmist view his own life compared to the wicked?

   Live for God, not ~~the~~ what others have

   d. What did he see in the wicked that made him think their lives were more meaningful than his? (verses 4–11)

   They had no trials

   e. How does he summarize the lives of the wicked? (verse 12)

   carefree

   f. What kind of life did the psalmist live? (verse 13)

   In vain

   g. What did he gain from his efforts? (verse 14)

   Punishment

   h. Compare the understanding of life described in verse 16 with that in verse 17.

   God opened their eyes to understand

   i. What ultimately gave meaning to his life? (verses 23–24)

   we will be in glory

   j. What is the surest foundation in this world? (verse 26)

   God is our strength

   k. Compare verse 28 with Ecclesiastes 12:13–14. How are the conclusions of the psalmist and Solomon similar?

   They fear God

2. How would you describe the meaning of life in general?

   To live with the love of God

   a. What do you believe is the specific purpose of your life?

   To love others and Tell them about God

b. How often do you find yourself echoing Solomon's sentiments of "What's the point?"

Several. The world is so wicked

c. What practices and disciplines keep you focused on your true purpose and calling in life?

Devotions, prayer, living

3. Read 1 Timothy 6:6–10.

a. How does godliness produce contentment? (verse 6)

We live for Christ

b. Why is it futile to attach meaning to the biggest, fastest, and newest that this world has to offer? (verse 7)

Human - we leave with nothing

c. How would it be possible for someone to find meaning in life if they possessed only food and clothing (and godliness)? (verse 8)

They wouldn't be in need.

d. How can finding contentment in money be a snare? (verse 9)

The love of money is destruction

e. What is the difference between "money" and "the love of money?" (verse 10)

Money to survive: Depend on money + not God

4. How content are you with the life you have at present? What would make you even more content?

Very Content. Family Salvation

DID YOU KNOW?

Sometimes we get so caught up in modern scientific achievements that we forget the intellectual powers of the ancients. Solomon was not the only one who observed nature and drew conclusions about this world. The wise men who visited Bethlehem at the birth of Jesus did so as a result of observing the movement of stars in the heavens (Matthew 2:2). And Jesus made reference to the common practice in His day of predicting the weather based on the color of the sky: "When it is evening you say, 'It will be fair weather, for the sky is red'; and in the morning, 'It will be foul weather today, for the sky is red and threatening.' Hypocrites! You know how to discern the face of the sky, but you cannot discern the signs of the times" (Matthew 16:2–3).

Sorting Out Your Life

Ecclesiastes 1:12–2:26

In this lesson we discover what does and does not satisfy in this life.

OUTLINE

People everywhere want to live a meaningful life; the question becomes how to find it. Some seek it in pleasure, some in knowledge, some in self-indulgence, some in work, and others in material things. Solomon discovered that meaning is found in none of those pursuits.

I. **The Experiences of Life Under the Sun**
   A. Searching for Meaning in Wisdom
   B. Searching for Meaning in Wild Living
   C. Searching for Meaning in Work
   D. Searching for Meaning in Wealth

II. **The Evaluation of Life Under the Sun**
   A. Man's Work Does Not Satisfy Him
   B. Man's Work Does Not Separate Him
   C. Man's Work Does Not Succeed Him

III. **The Enjoyment of Life Under the Sun**
   A. True Enjoyment Is a Gift From God
   B. True Enlightenment Is a Gift From God

OVERVIEW

We learned in the first lesson in this study that Solomon is near the end of his life, looking back over his shoulder, recounting his fruitless search for meaning and purpose apart from God. Three key words tell the story of his search: "vanity," meaning emptiness or uselessness; "under the sun," referring to life in this world apart from God; and "profit" meaning that which is left over.

THE EXPERIENCES OF LIFE UNDER THE SUN (1:12–2:10)

In this section of Ecclesiastes, Solomon examines his search for meaning from four perspectives: wisdom, wild living, work, and wealth.

Searching for Meaning in Wisdom (1:12–18)

A few years ago, Dr. James Dobson recounted the story of a teenage girl in Fremont, California, who achieved a perfect score on her SAT tests and a perfect score on the University of California acceptance tests—the first person ever to do so. She was a straight A student in high school who considered herself a typical teenager. But her teachers called her Wonder Woman because of her studious habits and photographic memory. In an interview with a reporter, when she was asked, "What is the meaning of life?" she replied, "I have no idea. I would like to know myself."

Here was a brilliant, educated teenager whose great learning had not produced the meaning of life. The late philosopher and author, Dr. Frances Schaeffer, said, "The damnation of this generation is that it doesn't know that it has any meaning at all." Solomon, the wisest man who ever lived, said, "For in much wisdom is much grief, and he who increases knowledge increases sorrow" (verse 1:18).

If education could bring meaning and purpose in life, then Ph.D.'s would be the happiest, most fulfilled people in the world. Education, even wisdom, is not the source of meaning and purpose in life.

Searching for Meaning in Wild Living (2:1–3)

Next, Solomon tells about trying to find meaning through pleasure and self-indulgent living. Given Solomon's wealth and the peace that Israel enjoyed during his reign as king, he had plenty of opportunity to seek meaning in wild living.

1. He tried amusement (2:1–2).

   Solomon tried amusement, mirth, pleasure, and laughter, but found them all wanting: "Madness! . . . What does it accomplish?" (2:2) He was trying to make happiness an end in itself, which is a futile endeavor. In Proverbs 14:13 he wrote, "Even in laughter the heart may sorrow, and the end of mirth may be grief."

   We can imagine Solomon's royal palace being like a Las Vegas hotel during this period, filled with a "bright lights, big city" atmosphere. Many today have tried what Solomon tried to dull the ache of meaninglessness through wanton living. And they have found what he found: There is no meaning in amusement.

2. He tried alcohol (2:3).

   Solomon didn't become an alcoholic or a drunkard. He kept his senses about him so he could record his experiments with wine and pleasure. But even after incorporating alcohol into his pursuit for meaning, he discovered it, too, was a vain pursuit. His stomach might have been full, but his heart was still empty.

Searching for Meaning in Work (2:4–6)

Wisdom and wild living didn't change Solomon's life, so he decided to throw himself into his work. In verses 4–6 Solomon uses the pronoun "I," "my," or "myself" ten times. All the building programs he undertook—houses, vineyards, gardens, orchards—were oriented around his own need to find meaning. But they turned out to have little effect.

When I returned recently to the college where my father invested 50 years as president and chancellor, I discovered that the current and retiring president had overseen the building of a hundred million dollars of new facilities on the campus. While those new buildings will ably serve students and faculty and the community, there is no ultimate meaning attached to them. They are just bricks and mortar that will crumble in time. Unless buildings are linked to the glory of God (which those at Cedarville College are), they are only monuments to man with no eternal significance. Solomon discovered that work projects, unless done for God, do not bring lasting meaning.

Work has meaning in the short term, but not in an eternal sense. Work is a means to an end, not an end in itself. We cannot work or build enough to fill the eternal shape of the human heart.

When Ernest Hemingway, one of the twentieth century's most famous authors, died, he left a sad suicide note. After having lived a life full of every adventure one could imagine, this "man's man" concluded, "Life is just one damn thing after another." Solomon would probably have agreed with Hemingway.

We can find people throughout history who have sought meaning through accomplishments. Old Testament commentator Derek Kidner has identified the problem with such a strategy: "What spoils the pleasures of life for us is our hunger to get out of them more than they can ever deliver." Work was not designed by God to be an ultimate source of meaning.

Searching for Meaning in Wealth (2:7–10)

Solomon's last target for finding meaning was in his vast wealth, which he had more of than anyone else in the world. Solomon's wealth, in today's dollar amounts, would have been staggering (1 Kings 10:14). Solomon's drinking goblets and the vessels in his house were all made of pure gold. Solomon had so much gold that silver was considered inferior (1 Kings 10:21). Rulers from all the world sent him tributes of gold and other forms of wealth, and his own fleet of trading ships brought back treasures from other lands. Solomon's palace and personal life dripped with the accouterments of wealth.

Solomon would have agreed with a writer in the *Wall Street Journal:* "[Money is] an article which may be used [as a] universal passport to everywhere except heaven and a universal provider of everything except happiness."

Cecil Rhodes left England, went to South Africa at age 27 and founded the DeBeers Mining Company. He soon controlled the entire South African diamond industry and became Prime Minister at age 36. Probably the richest man in the world at the time of his death, Rhodes was also a close personal friend of General William Booth, founder of the Salvation Army. On one occasion, General Booth asked Rhodes, "Tell me, man, are you happy?" Rhodes looked at Booth and said, "Happy? Me? Good heavens, no!"

Solomon and Rhodes both learned that a life lived without reference to God is empty regardless of how much money you have.

The Evaluation of Life Under the Sun (2:11–23)

Solomon makes three evaluations of the experiments he pursued with wisdom, wild living, work, and wealth.

Man's Work Does Not Satisfy Him (2:11–12)

Verses 11–12 summarize Solomon's conclusion that work doesn't fill the bill. Man was created by God to be satisfied by God, and no amount of counterfeit efforts to find meaning in life will be successful. In all his works, "there was no profit under the sun" (verse 2:11).

Man's Work Does Not Separate Him (2:13–16)

Solomon makes a subtle argument in verses 13–16, and it is this: You never see a U-Haul trailer attached to a hearse. When you die, everything you have done and accumulated stays right here. You can't take it with you.

Regardless of whether you've been wise or foolish in life, there is no separation between the two at death if there is no God. If this life under the sun is all there is, then there is no difference between the wise and the foolish. We all die and that's all there is.

Man's Work Does Not Succeed Him (2:18–23)

Solomon's third evaluation is that man's work does not succeed him. What you do in this life stays in this life when you die. You have no control over who gets the benefit of all you've done.

Solomon is driving stakes into the ego of man in these verses; he is pulling the rug out from under us. All that we think we have done that is great is forgotten at death. When you die, all your work—your money, your bank accounts, your resources—is turned over to somebody else to manage. You did the work and someone else reaps the rewards. Death is the leveler that brings us back to reality: None of our work has lasting significance unless it is tied to the glory of God in some way. But work for work's sake is meaningless and vain.

Our goal as Christians is to set our affections on things above, not things on this earth.

The Enjoyment of Life Under the Sun (2:24–26)

Solomon discovers that part of the meaning of life is to live and enjoy it as a gift from God.

True Enjoyment Is a Gift From God (2:24–25)

A better translation of verse 25 is, "Who can eat, or who can have enjoyment without God?" We can try to find pleasure in life without God, but ultimately we can't.

Eight times in Ecclesiastes Solomon makes reference to eating and drinking and enjoying life. His point is that we need to understand life under the sun for what it is and not confuse it with what it's not. It's not the ultimate, but it is something that can be enjoyed as a gift from God. Solomon doesn't translate his inability to find ultimate meaning in life into a dark morbidity about life. He says enjoy it to the extent it is enjoyable. While true and permanent joy is found only in God, life offers a measure of enjoyment of which we should not be afraid to take advantage.

Solomon does away with the idea that God is some kind of cosmic kill-joy. When we seek ultimate joy in this world, we don't find it; but when we learn to enjoy this world that God has created, everything comes into proper perspective. If you are a person who believes God is against your enjoying life, you need to adopt Solomon's perspective. Life can be a great source of joy when we learn to view it against the backdrop of God who created life and gives it as a gift to His creation.

Whatever God has given you in life, hold it with an open hand. Allow God to take from your hand to bless others and to give back to your hand even more than you have. View life as a gift from God, and you will learn to enjoy it under His direction and blessing (1 Timothy 6:17). God is not like drugs or alcohol where you have to take more to continue to get pleasure or stimulus. Instead of being increasingly dissatisfied with God, you are increasingly satisfied the better you get to know Him and the more you enjoy His gifts.

True Enlightenment Is a Gift From God (2:26)

I know two families, both of whom own beautiful homes. One family just hordes their house. They hardly use it for fear of marring its perfection. It is an idol of sorts to them. The other family is constantly trying to think of how to use their house for the glory of God. They constantly have missionaries staying with them and use it for other ministry functions. The latter family seems to really enjoy their house while the first family doesn't. Enlightenment about the use of God's gifts and the enjoyment of life comes from God.

Solomon says that to some, God gives the work of "gathering and collecting, that he may give to him who is good before God." We can either be the gatherer and collector or the one who is receiving the gifts. There is work and blessing being stored up for the righteous as a gift from God (Proverbs 13:22). Someone asked me once whether, if they won the lottery, they should give part of the money to God. First I told them they shouldn't be using God's money to gamble on the lottery, but if they did come into a large sum of money such as from the lottery, of course they should give part to God! That's a perfect illustration of how money is transferred by God to accomplish His purposes.

There is a way to have joy and fulfillment in life, but it won't be found in this world. It will be found in the God who made this world and gives it to us as a gift to enjoy.

Isaiah 55:1–3 summarizes this section of Ecclesiastes well:

"Ho! Everyone who thirsts,
Come to the waters;
And you who have no money,
Come, buy and eat.
Yes, come, buy wine and milk
Without money and without price.
Why do you spend money for *what is* not bread,
And your wages for *what* does not satisfy?
Listen carefully to Me, and eat *what* is good,
And let your soul delight itself in abundance.
Incline your ear, and come to Me.
Hear, and your soul shall live;
And I will make an everlasting covenant with you—
The sure mercies of David.

APPLICATION

1. In his earlier years, Solomon wrote about the benefits of wisdom in Proverbs. Note the benefits of wisdom as found in the following passages:

   a. 3:13–15

   b. 3:16

   c. 3:17–18

   d. 4:7–9

   e. 8:32–36

   f. What is the difference between how Solomon discusses wisdom in Proverbs and how he portrays it in Ecclesiastes?

   g. What is the proper context for wisdom, knowledge, and education in life?

   h. Is it better to be uneducated and fear God or be educated and not fear God? Why? (see Proverbs 1:7; 9:10)

2. What did Solomon say about alcohol in these passages from Proverbs?

   a. 20:1

   b. 23:20–21

c. 23:29–30

d. 31:4–5

e. What is the meaning of Proverbs 31:6?

f. Explain your own conviction regarding alcohol.

3. Read 1 Corinthians 1:18–2:10
   a. What is the ultimate end of human wisdom and intelligence? (verse 19)

   b. Why does God work to make the wisdom of man foolishness? What does this mean? (verses 20–21)

   c. Explain how verse 25 is true.

   d. Instead of human intelligence, what did the apostle Paul rely on? (verse 2:2)

   e. What is the source of true wisdom? (verses 2:6–10)

4. Read 1 Timothy 6:17.
   a. What is the purpose of all God has given to us?

   b. At what point does wealth become a problem?

   c. How can one integrate wealth into a lifestyle of joy in God?

5. What do you learn about joy from Acts 13:49–52?

   a. What would the world's perspective on this situation be?

   b. In what context does Paul describe joy in Romans 14:17?

   c. What examples of worldly pursuits does he cite as not being the source of joy?

   d. Who is the source of true joy in Romans 15:13?

   e. What striking contrast do you find concerning joy in 2 Corinthians 8:2?

   f. Who is the source of joy in 1 Thessalonians 1:6?

DID YOU KNOW?

The two primary names for God in the Old Testament are the words *Elohim* and *Yahweh. Elohim* is a Hebrew word that doesn't refer specifically to the God of Israel but to gods of any sort. *Yahweh,* however, is the personal name of Israel's God, first revealed to Moses on Mount Sinai (Exodus 3:13–15). Solomon's spiritual deterioration can be tracked from his writing of Proverbs, where he referred to God by His personal name, *Yahweh,* more than 80 times, to Ecclesiastes where he doesn't use *Yahweh* at all. Instead, in Ecclesiastes, Solomon refers to God by the non-personal name, *Elohim.*

Beautiful in His Time

Ecclesiastes 3:1–15

In this lesson we learn that God's plans and purposes rule over the affairs of this world.

OUTLINE

No one would choose a difficult time over an easy time, but everyone has some of both in this life. The challenge in life is not to eliminate the hard times, but to develop a deep confidence that there is a time and purpose for everything, that God's plan's are, while mysterious, still good.

I. Some Impressions About Life
- A. How Time Affects Our Body
- B. How Time Affects Our Soul
- C. How Time Affects Our Spirit

II. Some Insights About God
- A. His Plan Is Good
- B. His Purpose Is Clear
- C. His Program Is Mysterious

III. Some Instructions About Living
- A. Don't Forfeit Enjoyment Because of What You Can't Understand
- B. Don't Forget to Be Thankful for God's Gifts to You
- C. Don't Fear Life; Fear God

OVERVIEW

Rabbi Harold Kushner wrote a book titled *When Bad Things Happen to Good People,* in which he told the tragic story of his young son's death from a debilitating disease. As a religious person, he wrestled with why God allowed such a thing to happen. He concluded one of two things must be true: Either God is all-loving, but not all-powerful (He wants to prevent disease but can't) or God is all-powerful, but not all-loving (He is able to prevent disease but won't).

The conclusion the rabbi came to was the first of the two options: God is loving but not omnipotent. God cares about us, but has decided to let the world run on its own without intervention from Him. God is not sovereign or all-powerful; He keeps His distance from the everyday affairs of this world.

After my own bout with cancer, I debated a disciple of Rabbi Kushner on the topic of suffering, and he echoed Kushner's position: We shouldn't pray to be healed because, since God has nothing to do with the cause of illness, we shouldn't expect Him to be involved in its removal.

Solomon would not agree with Rabbi Kushner's conclusions. He believed that God is sovereign over all of time and history and that nothing happens outside of His purposes—including suffering.

In this section of Ecclesiastes, Solomon offers impressions about life, insights about God, and instructions about living which touch the issues of pain and suffering in this life.

Some Impressions About Life (3:1–8)

Solomon begins with fourteen couplets—28 statements about life, 14 negative and 14 positive—which fall into three categories about time and its relationship to body, soul, and spirit. He mentions "time" 29 times as well as other time-related concepts such as seasons, eternity, and forever.

How Time Affects Our Body (3:2–3)

He begins by affirming that there is a time for "every purpose under heaven" (verse 1), which certainly includes a time to be born and a time to die. And those aren't random times—they are times known by God.

When one of my grandsons was born, I remember thinking as I stood looking at him in the hospital nursery that in another room in the same hospital a life was probably ending. Life begins and life ends; there is a time to be born and a time to die. Nurseries and morgues have a constant stream of human beings passing through them as life begins and ends. Life has its seasons.

In the same vein, there is a time to plant and a time to harvest—seasons which every farmer and every gardener knows. And there are seasons of killing and seasons of healing. Scientists tell us our body is completely rebuilt every seven years as our trillions of cells die off and are replaced. There are times to break down and times to build up. We are built up in our youth and we begin breaking down in our old age. It's the natural cycle of life.

Time definitely affects our bodies. We are born, and we die; we are built up, and we wear down; we sow, and we reap. And God is involved in all of those seasons of life. God is not outside of our lives—He is intimately involved in every aspect, even death and suffering. God is all-loving and all-powerful. If He doesn't prevent pain and suffering, it is not because He is impotent; it is because His purposes are otherwise.

How Time Affects Our Soul (3:4–5)

Time also affects our soul, the emotional part of our life. There is a time to weep, to laugh, to mourn, and to dance. These emotions are common to every person in the world, and there is a time for each in the seasons of life we go through. At the two opposite ends of the spectrum, there is a time for weeping and a time for rejoicing. Both are in God's plan.

There are also times for affirmation and times for distancing, casting away and gathering, embracing and refraining. God is in all these emotional times as well. God is not in the good times alone, but in the hard times as well.

How Time Affects Our Spirit (3:6–8)

The last six couplets have to do with the inner man . . . the spiritual experiences of life. We gain, we lose; we keep, we throw away; we tear, we sew; we speak, we keep quiet; we love, we hate; we enjoy peace, we go to war.

Life is a changing of seasons in the spiritual realm. We go through periods of accumulation, and then we decide to pare down. We have garage sales and start throwing or giving things away. Why? Because there are times when we have a need for both aspects of life.

Some wonder how there could be a time for hate. Jesus hated. He hated sin . . . injustice . . . corruption . . . destruction. And we need to learn to hate the same things He hated. There are times and seasons for us to be radical in our pursuit of righteousness and our abolition of injustice. We must love the sinner (for example, the abortion doctor) but hate the sin (the murder of unborn children). There is a time to love and to hate. Sometimes that translates into a time for war. We wish for peace at all times, but sometimes evil must be confronted and defeated.

Solomon is saying that all of life unfolds under the divine appointment of Providence. Nothing happens randomly or arbitrarily. There are times and seasons for everything under heaven. We may not like that fact, and certainly can't fully explain it, but it is biblical truth from the pen of the wisest man who ever lived.

How powerful would a God be who was not in control over everything? By definition, God is over all things at both ends of every spectrum and everything in between as well.

Does God promote evil? Is He responsible for sin? No! God is not the author of anything evil or wicked, but He is certainly in control of it all. His permissive will allows whatever His directive will does not cause. God does not edit out the unpleasant parts of life, for it is through trials that our faith is strengthened and our character is built. One day all suffering will be eliminated from planet earth; but until that time, we live with all the seasons of life. Our lives are lived according to His plan, not ours. He is in control of the times and seasons of our lives.

Some Insights About God (3:9–15)

Who is this God who allows both the good and the bad in life? Solomon next answers that question with three key insights about the God who is over the times and seasons of life.

His Plan Is Good (3:9–11a)

Solomon begins by asking, in essence, "What's the point?" After all the seasons of life come and go—we build up only to have it torn down—what profit remains? Solomon says that we become so busy with life that we fail to understand the meaning of it unless we stop and ponder this one fact: "He made everything beautiful in its time." In other words, God's plan is good; everything that happens, happens for a purpose. This is the Old Testament equivalent of Romans 8:28.

We have no problem believing that the good things in life are beautiful in their time, such as meeting the love of our life. But 10 or 15 years into the marriage, we may not think things are as beautiful as they once were. We believe health is beautiful, but not cancer. We have to realize that life is life, and everything is part of God's good plan.

Consider the words of Malcolm Muggeridge, the British journalist who became a devoted Christian:

"Contrary to what might be expected, I look back on experiences that at the time seemed especially desolating and painful, with particular satisfaction. Indeed, I can say with complete truthfulness that everything that has truly enhanced and enlightened my existence has been through affliction and not through happiness, whether pursued or attained. In other words, if it ever were to be possible to eliminate affliction from our earthly existence by means of some drug or other medical mumbo jumbo, as Aldous Huxley envisaged in *Brave New World*, the result would not be to make life delectable, but to make it too banal and trivial to be endurable. This, of course, is what the Cross signifies. And it is the Cross, more than anything else, that has called me inexorably to Christ."

All the painful things that happen in life—the Holocaust, 9-11, the tragic death of a person in the prime of life—either drive us to God or away from God. Biblically, they should drive us to Him since Solomon teaches us that everything happens in its time, meaning God's plan is good.

His Purpose Is Clear (3:11b)

When Solomon says that God has put eternity in our hearts, it means we have a longing inside us for something more than we will ever gain from this world. Even after coming to know God, we still long to be free from the trappings of this world (Romans 8:22). Professor Walter Kaiser puts it this way: "Man has an inborn inquisitiveness and capacity to learn how everything in his experience can be integrated to make a whole. He wants to know how the mundane 'downstairs' realm of ordinary, day-to-day living fits with the 'upstairs' realm of the here-after. . . ."

St. Augustine said, "Thou has made us for Thyself, and our hearts are restless until they learn to rest in Thee." And C. S. Lewis put it this way: "Our Heavenly Father has provided many delightful inns for us along our journey, but He takes great care to see that we do not mistake any of them for home." Our hearts know the difference between a temporary and permanent home.

His Program Is Mysterious (3:11c)

Good and mysterious are summarized by the fact that "no one can find out the work that God does from beginning to end." No one can figure out God's plan on his own.

If you embraced Christianity thinking you would be provided the answers to all of life's mysterious and painful questions, you will be disappointed. God's plan is good and His purpose is clear, but those plans and purposes remain a mystery at some level. God is God and He doesn't owe us an answer or an explanation for what He does. The secret things belong to Him (Deuteronomy 29:29).

Some Instructions About Living (3:12–13)

Finally, Solomon gives us three instructions about living in light of what we know about life and what we know about God.

Don't Forfeit Enjoyment Because of What You Can't Understand (3:12)

Don't spend your life trying to figure out what God is doing. If you do, you'll miss the great joy that life has to offer which comes from God as a gift. I think a lot of Christians, in the sunset of their life, are going to look back and wish they had enjoyed life more. Somehow we have the idea that God expects us to work and minister diligently, and that if we're enjoying ourselves, we must not be working or ministering hard enough! If you can't enjoy life because you're hung up on what you don't understand about life . . . well, that's your fault, not God's.

Don't Forget to Be Thankful for God's Gifts to You (3:13)

When I hear people complaining about their job, I want to remind them to be thankful that they have a job at all. Solomon says we ought to "eat and drink and enjoy the good of all [our] labor," which we do as a result of being able to work. Everything is a gift from God for which we ought to be thankful (1 Chronicles 29:10–15). Sometimes we get so caught up in what we don't like about life that we forget to be thankful for life itself.

Don't Fear Life; Fear God (3:14–15)

God is in control, and His plans and purposes will stand. Instead of fearing or complaining about life, we ought to fear God; for what

He decides is what will happen. We can neither add to nor take away from God's plan, which makes Him worth fearing (respecting, honoring). The next time something about life confuses you, instead of it being a stumbling block, let it remind you that God is God and you're not. Be thankful He will never leave you nor forsake you even when you are confused and lack understanding (Hebrews 13:5).

Let the same attitude be in you that was in Christ Jesus who was treated more unfairly and painfully than anyone in history (Philippians 2:5–11). You can rejoice in all the times and seasons of your life because God makes them all beautiful in His time.

APPLICATION

1. Write down instances in your life where there was . . .
   a. a time to sow followed by a time to reap
   b. a time to break down and a time to build up
   c. a time to weep and a time to laugh
   d. a time to mourn and a time to celebrate
   e. a time to gain and a time to lose
   f. a time to speak and a time to refrain from speaking
   g. a time to express love and a time to express hatred
2. Read Psalm 139:16.
   a. When did God first begin to know you?
   b. What do "days" and "your book" suggest about God's knowledge of your life?
   c. Do you believe God looked ahead and saw what would happen in your life and that He wrote it down? Explain.

d. What comfort does this verse provide in time of difficulty in the present?

e. How many of the "times" in Ecclesiastes 3:1–8 does this verse cover?

3. What does Lamentations 3:37–38 suggest about God's power and oversight?

   a. What about Ephesians 1:11?

   b. And Daniel 2:21?

4. Read James 1:2–5.

   a. When you encounter negative "times," what does James say you should do? (verse 2)

   b. What are the advantages of the negative times? (verse 3)

   c. What is the ultimate reason God allows the negative times? (verse 4)

   d. What discipline should you employ when you are confused about what God has allowed? (verse 5)

5. Read Romans 5:3–5.
   a. What does suffering lead to? (verse 3)

   b. What does perseverance produce? (verse 4a)

   c. What does character produce? (verse 4b)

   d. What is the advantage of having hope? (verse 5)

   e. Therefore, what should you do when you suffer? (verse 3a)

DID YOU KNOW?

Ecclesiastes falls into the category of books in the Bible that are primarily written as Hebrew poetry or songs (the others being Job, Psalms, Proverbs, and Song of Solomon). Ecclesiastes 3:2–8 is written as couplets, units of verse consisting of two lines which usually rhyme, have the same meter, and contain a unity of thought. In our English Bibles, each of the seven verses contains two couplets, making 14 in all. Among his other attributes, Solomon was a master of poetic verse. Proverbs is written in the form of (mostly) short sayings (Hebrew *mashal,* to be like), and Song of Solomon is written as a love poem or song.

When Your World Doesn't Make Sense

Ecclesiastes 3:16–4:16

In this lesson we learn that life's biggest problems are not ours to solve.

OUTLINE

Our local and global problems seem overwhelming, yet Solomon faced them as well. What do we do about sweeping injustice and various forms of oppression? Solomon says to stay focused on God who will ultimately balance the scales, right the wrongs, and erase inconsistencies.

I. The Problem of Faulty Justice
- A. What Solomon Saw
- B. What Solomon Said

II. The Problem of Fierce Oppression

III. The Problem of Financial Rivalry

IV. The Problem of Fractured Relationships
- A. Riches Over Relationships
- B. Relationships Over Riches

V. The Problem of Fickle Popularity

OVERVIEW

Sometimes in life we are guilty of not seeing the forest for the trees, of missing something that is as clear as the nose on our face. Solomon does not allow us to do that in his book called Ecclesiastes. He tells us exactly how things are in the plainest of language.

So far we've learned there is no real meaning in life apart from God. We've also learned that there is a time and season for everything, that God's plans are good, His purpose is clear, but His program is sometimes mysterious. In this lesson, we are going to discover five aspects of life with which Solomon struggled. He speaks plainly and honestly, four times saying, "I saw . . . (3:16; 4:4, 7, 15).

Solomon is making observations about life and writing them down, calling them just as he sees them. Then he considers what he has observed: "I said in my heart . . . I perceived . . . I returned and considered." He is making observations and then pondering what he sees. His observations are an example of what is found in Ecclesiastes 12:11: "The words of the wise are like goads, and the words of scholars are like well-driven nails, given by one Shepherd."

A goad was a pointed stick that was used by a shepherd to keep sheep in line as they moved along a road. Solomon's questions and observations are like goads from God, the "one Shepherd," that He uses to move us along in life. The issues Solomon raises in this section are not easy ones, but they will force us out of our zone of comfort into the way of God's wisdom.

The Problem of Faulty Justice (3:16–22)

Solomon's first goad has to do with faulty justice—a problem in our day as well as his.

What Solomon Saw (3:16)

Solomon saw injustice in the tribunals of his day—the guilty went free and the innocent suffered unjustly. The rich could buy their freedom, the poor were abused by the system. If God is good, where is the justice?

What Solomon Said (3:17–22)

Solomon has three observations to make about this lack of justice:

1. Judgment is coming (3:17).

   Solomon believes a time is coming when "God shall judge the righteous and the wicked (verse 17). Just because we don't see justice now doesn't mean it will never prevail (Ecclesiastes 8:6). The innocent will be recompensed and the guilty will be punished. The lack of judgment now encourages some to think they can get away with injustice (Ecclesiastes 8:11), but the day is coming when the scales will be balanced.

2. Death is certain (3:18–21).

   Solomon's second point is that death is certain. Critics of the Bible love these verses because they think Solomon means that death is the last act—there's nothing after death. But that is not Solomon's point. He is saying that, while it appears the rich and powerful have the upper hand when it comes to justice, they will die just like the animals. They cannot escape death and the judgment that follows.

   Solomon is not talking about the spirit of man, but the body of man. Death is the great leveler for all living beings, man and animal. The privileged in this life have no privileges when it comes to death. All end up in the grave. There is a difference in man and animals, however. The spirit of man goes upward ("to God who gave it"; Ecclesiastes 12:7) and the spirit of the animal goes down to the earth. Man is not just a higher form of animal, Solomon says. Though death is the constant for all, man returns to the God who made him.

3. Life continues (3:22).

   A third goad or nail Solomon drives home is that life goes on in spite of injustice. We are not to stop living life because we can't fix every injustice we see. Death and the judgment to follow will remedy what we can't change in this life. Between now and the judgment, we are to rejoice in our work and continue on with life (verse 22).

   Solomon reminds us again that the answers to the puzzles in life are not ours to figure out. We are to live and rejoice in the life God has given and trust Him for what we don't and can't know.

The Problem of Fierce Oppression (4:1–3)

Faulty justice was Solomon's first question, and his second deals with fierce oppression. He sees the weak and helpless of the world who are victimized by society. He sees their tears and lack of comfort. Who are the oppressed to turn to? Where is God in the lives of the oppressed?

Simon Weisenthal, a Holocaust survivor, wrote in his book about his experience that he stopped believing in God when he saw how his fellow Jews were tortured and oppressed in the concentration camps: "When I saw the oppression and the wickedness and the injustice of that, I couldn't comprehend it, and I turned from God." Solomon says, from a purely human perspective, the oppressed would be better off having never been born than to suffer evil and oppression in this world. Job expressed the same sentiment in the midst of his suffering (Job 3:3, 11).

Solomon's father, King David, wrestled with the world's inequities and found answers only when he "went into the sanctuary of God; then I understood . . ." (Psalm 73:17). Trying to understand the events of this world and the purposes of God with your own wisdom is fruitless. Only in the presence of God do we find relief for the tension we feel living with this life's unanswered questions. This is not a passive cop out. The passive approach would be to pretend problems don't exist, to deny reality. But God is the greatest reality we have, so we take real questions to a real God and leave them with Him.

The Problem of Financial Rivalry (4:4–6)

Solomon's third goad deals with the envy and grasping for material advantage that goes on in this world. Greed and pride of possession were as common in his day as they are in ours. Men work not to meet their needs, but to be able to own something bigger and better than their neighbor, to be the envy of their friends. The search for power and financial advantage is as active on Main Street as it is on Wall Street—not to mention in the halls of government where power is king.

In verse 5 Solomon says, "The fool folds his hands and consumes his own flesh." Some people react negatively to the search for financial advantage and drop out of the system. That happened in America in the 1960s and 1970s. But Solomon says dropping out is not the answer any more than striving for advantage is. The "hippies" of the 1960s didn't find any answers, but they did consume a decade of their lives in futile efforts to reform a system they didn't like.

Solomon says there is a better way: "Better a handful with quietness than both hands full, together with toil and grasping for the wind" (verse 6). He's talking about balance. You don't have to have it all, but you have to have some in order to live. So get "a handful" and leave the scraping and clawing, or the dropping out, to those on the extremes. The Bible is filled with admonitions to living in balance when it comes to material things (Proverbs 15:16; 16:8; 30:7–9; 1 Timothy 6:6–8).

The Problem of Fractured Relationships (4:7–12)

Solomon's fourth goad has to do with fractured relationships—he sees many who are alone in the world.

Riches Over Relationships (4:7–8)

Solomon sees people working themselves to death, toiling to amass more and more wealth. They have no friends or relatives with whom to share their wealth. They are like Charles Dickens' Scrooge character—alone in the world with only his money to keep him company.

Relationships Over Riches (4:9–12)

In verses 9–12 Solomon warns against sacrificing relationships for riches. Relationships are always the priority. We aren't to use people to get things, we are to use things to encourage and minister to people. Money and materials are means to an end, not the end in themselves.

Solomon gives us four reasons why having friends is better than not having friends:

1. Two are better than one for working (4:9).

   Sharing the burden of labor is always easier and more fun when you are working with another instead of by yourself. Synergy happens: The whole is greater than the sum of its parts. Two can accomplish more and share a greater reward than either could alone.

2. Two are better than one for walking (4:10).

   Friends provide help in times of trouble. Being alone in dark and troubling times is discouraging. Friends can encourage us to continue on in the face of obstacles.

3. Two are better than one for warmth (4:11).

   People in ancient times, sleeping in the open while traveling, would huddle together for warmth. But this is also a good word for marriage—a lifelong companion provides warmth in body, soul, and spirit.

4. Two are better than one for watch-care (4:12).

   There is safety in numbers. This was definitely true in the physical world of biblical days when protection was an issue. But it can also be true in our day when we need protection spiritually and emotionally as well as physically.

In all four of these examples, Solomon is saying, "Don't destroy your relationships and the benefits of them for the sake of pursuing riches. You will regret it down the road when you find yourself alone."

The Problem of Fickle Popularity (4:13–16)

There has been no small amount of discussion concerning the meaning of these verses. I believe Solomon is looking back in history to his own family in order to talk about fickle popularity. I believe the "old and foolish king" (verse 13) is Saul, the first king of Israel, who was selected by the people of Israel because of his charismatic personality. He started out with everything and ended up with nothing, consulting a witch instead of God (1 Samuel 28:7 ff.; 1 Chronicles 10:13).

Saul was replaced by a "poor and wise youth" (verse 13) whom I believe to be David, Solomon's father. Raised as a shepherd boy, David was anointed to replace Saul because of what God saw in his heart (1 Samuel 16:7). Solomon says that a shepherd boy, born in humble circumstances, is a better choice for king than an old and foolish man who refuses to submit to the Lord.

Who was the "second youth who stands in his place" (verse 15)? I believe Solomon is here referring to himself. He was crowned with great fanfare, and he ruled over a large nation. Yet "those who come afterward will not rejoice in him" (verse 16).

With these examples, Solomon is referring to the fickleness of popularity. Everyone loved Saul, then everyone loved David, then everyone loved him. The crowds sang about how "Saul has slain his thousands, and David his ten thousands" (1 Samuel 18:7). Then Solomon took the throne, and everyone hailed him as Israel's new king.

Popularity is fickle and fleeting and is not something to be depended on: "Surely this also is vanity and grasping for the wind" (verse 16). Solomon is warning against the inconsistencies of popularity. He doesn't understand it, but he realizes it is part of life in this world. It is not something that should ruin or wreck one's life. It is a fact of life that we live with. Ask yourself this: Who won any number of awards last year? The Oscars? The Super Bowl? Baseball's MVP? Gold medals in the last Olympics?

Some people track those awards because it's their business or a personal interest, but most people don't know. We celebrate when they happen, then forget and move on to the next hot topic. That's just the way life is. Everyone has a short attention span when it comes to who's hot and who's not. And we should have a short attention span about our own popularity as well. Enjoy it while you can because it probably won't last long. Popularity should never become a goal for the person who wants to be consistently happy. People are fickle, but God is not. You can be popular with Him forever.

With all of these issues—faulty justice, fierce oppression, financial rivalry, fractured relationships, fierce popularity—Solomon is trying to turn us toward God. He is speaking with the wisdom of hindsight. He succumbed to the futility of dealing with some of these issues in his life, but he doesn't want his readers to. God is the only certainty in life. He knows the answers to all these issues even when we don't. To allow our lives to get derailed over issues we cannot fix or even understand is "vanity and grasping for the wind."

APPLICATION

1. What do you learn about injustice and oppression in the Old Testament from the following passages?

   a. Isaiah 1:23

   b. Isaiah 10:1–2

   c. Amos 2:6

   d. Amos 5:7

   e. Micah 2:1–2

   f. Malachi 3:5

2. What are the most serious injustices you see happening in your community, our nation, or the world?

   a. Will they ever be totally eliminated?

   b. How do you find a balance as a Christian between trying or not trying to correct something that you know will never be eliminated?

   c. Why won't injustice and oppression ever be done away with in this world?

3. Read Ezekiel 34.
    a. How were Israel's rulers mistreating those for whom they had responsibility? (verses 1–9)

    b. What was God's response in behalf of the oppressed? (verses 10–16, 20–31)

4. What kind of future judgment is described in 1 Corinthians 3:11–14?

    a. Is this a judgment of Christians or non-Christians?

    b. How does Paul describe this setting in Romans 14:10 and 2 Corinthians 5:10?

5. Read Revelation 20:11–15.
    a. What does the throne in this setting signify? (verse 11)

    b. Who was standing before the throne? (verse 12)

    c. What does "small and great" indicate? (verse 12)

    d. What book was opened as the basis for judgment? (verse 12)

    e. What was the basis of judgment? Faith or works? (verse 12–13)

f. How do you know that Christians are not involved in this judgment? (Romans 8:1)

g. What happened to anyone whose name was not found in the Book of Life?

h. How would you summarize (from Romans 2:1–16) the basis of God's judgment on those who don't know Christ?

6. What does Agur ask of God concerning material possessions? (Proverbs 30:7–9)

a. How do you respond to his request? Would you pray the same prayer?

b. Do you consider yourself as having little, a lot, or in the middle?

c. For what are you striving materially in your life?

DID YOU KNOW?

We often speak of "man and the animals" but in truth, man is classed in the group *Mammalia* along with the brute beasts. If we want to draw broad distinctions, it should be between the animal kingdom and the plant kingdom. This is most clearly seen in Genesis 1:29–30 where the animal kingdom is given the plant kingdom for food. Yet there is a distinction between man and beasts, and that is the image of God (*imago Dei;* Genesis 1:26–27). Both beasts and man share "the breath of life" (Hebrew *nephesh;* Genesis 2:7; 7:15) but only man was selected of all the animals to bear the image of God.

Taking Your Troubles to Church

Ecclesiastes 5:1–20

In this lesson we learn four things not to do when troubles come.

OUTLINE

You've heard "there are no atheists in foxholes." Meaning, when the battle heats up, we're eager to do a deal with God. If that doesn't work, we're quick to blame Him—or the government. Or wish we could buy our way out of trouble. All of these are vanity, Solomon says.

I. **Don't Blame God for Your Situation**
   A. Walk Carefully Before Him
   B. Talk Cautiously to Him

II. **Don't Bribe God With a Vow**

III. **Don't Be Surprised at the Government's Response**

IV. **Don't Believe the Lie About Riches**
   A. Five Things You Should Know About Money
   B. Two Things You Need to Know About God

OVERVIEW

The week before I was to preach on Ecclesiastes 5:1–20 in our church, devastating wild fires swept through our county in California. A number of people in our church lost everything they owned, and the fires were within one mountain ridge of reaching our church campus, including our schools. But they were spared. I told my wife at the end of that week, "I am so glad I am a preacher of the Word of God." How else would we know how to respond to the devastation that sometimes comes upon us?

All of us experience tragedies and reversals in our lives at some point, and the principles in this section of Ecclesiastes will help you through those times just as they helped our church family recover from a devastating week.

Don't Blame God for Your Situation (5:1–3)

It is so easy to blame God when disaster strikes. But Solomon warns us to walk carefully before God and talk cautiously to God. We must measure our steps as well as our words before laying blame where it doesn't belong.

Walk Carefully Before Him (5:1)

We get our expression "Watch your step" from Solomon's words in verse one: "Walk prudently" (literally, "Keep your foot"). When we draw near to God, we are not to bring the sacrifice of fools. Don't act hastily or irrationally.

The purpose of coming into the house of God is to listen and learn, not to storm in with our agenda. Fear, reverence, and honor should characterize our attitude toward God when we draw near to Him. We should not make the mistake Saul made, thinking that outward worship could cover a disobedient heart. Instead of doing what God told him, Saul amended God's instructions. He let his agenda take precedence over God's (1 Samuel 15). As a result of his actions, the kingdom was taken from Saul; and David was anointed to replace him as king.

God's concluding words to Saul were, "Has the Lord as great delight in burnt offerings and sacrifices, as in obeying the voice of the Lord? Behold, to obey is better than sacrifice, and to heed than the fat of rams" (1 Samuel 15:22).

We are to be careful when we interact with God, that we walk carefully before Him, fully obeying what He expects us to do—and not blaming Him for things that happen which impact us negatively. In *Pilgrim's Progress,* John Bunyan wrote years ago, "In prayer, it is better to have a heart without words, than words without heart."

Talk Cautiously to Him (5:2–3)

These verses sound a lot like James in the New Testament: Be careful with your tongue! We are so quick to assign blame—yes, even blame God—when things go against us. God did not start the fire that burned near our home. In this particular case, the authorities believe an individual did. So why do we blame God?

As Christians, anytime we grouse and complain about life, we are blaming God. If we truly believe He is over all things, then it must be His fault that an inconsiderate driver cut me off on the freeway. Be careful about complaining. Directly or indirectly, you are blaming God for what has happened.

Solomon reminds us that God is in heaven and we are on earth. He sees everything, we see very little. If we knew everything God knows, we wouldn't complain and blame God as much as we do. If you had the ability to instantly trace back every cause and effect event leading up to the latest disaster in your life, you might be more careful about assigning blame. God sees all those events and knows why everything happened. We need to blame less and trust Him more.

Verse 3 suggests that we are sometimes fools—we babble on relentlessly like a man who has had dream after dream. We need to be careful with our speech, especially where God is concerned. Blaming God for things that go wrong is a dead-end street that goes nowhere—except to further confusion and despair.

Don't Bribe God With a Vow (5:4–7)

Have you ever made a deal with God in the face of impending doom? "Lord, please spare me and I'll become a missionary." It's why they say there are no atheists in foxholes. When the battle gets heavy, everybody wants to play "Let's Make a Deal" with God. If you ever do make a commitment to God, make sure you keep it. And make sure it isn't an "I'll do this if You'll do that." Leave the deal-making to the politicians.

Here is Eugene Peterson's version of verses 6–7:

Don't let your mouth make a total sinner of you.
When called to account, you won't get by with
"Sorry, I didn't mean it."
Why risk provoking God to angry retaliation?
But against all illusion and fantasy and empty talk
There's always this rock foundation: Fear God!

It is far better to fear God than to speak rashly and have to explain ourselves later. Why does a difficult circumstance in life cause us to take back all that we have said we believe about God? There is no time like tragedy and difficulty to cast yourself totally on what you believe about God—His sovereignty and His goodness. The words that come out of our mouth cannot be retrieved and stuffed back in. Once they are spoken, we either have to shamefully repent or harden our heart against God.

I love what David said in the Psalms as he thought about a vow he had made. Psalm 66:13–14:

I will go into Your house with burnt offerings;
I will pay You my vows,
Which my lips have uttered
And my mouth has spoken when I was in trouble."

Vows in times of trouble were common in the Old Testament, and here we see David keeping his vow. But there must have been plenty of instances where people didn't keep them as evidenced by Solomon's words. Remember: Don't make deals with God and if you make a promise, keep it.

Don't Be Surprised at the Government's Response (5:8-9)

You may be surprised at the heading for this section, but I am not making this up. Solomon warns his readers about the actions of government officials. In short, don't be surprised when you see injustice and inequity in government.

It seems the government gets blamed today for almost everything. Next to God, they get blamed the most, sometimes inappropriately. If we take Solomon's advice, we won't be so surprised when the government helps itself more than they help those they are supposed to serve. As for corruption in the government (at least in Solomon's day), "There's no end to it, and nothing can be done about it" (verse 8, *The Message*).

The government's problem is the same as mine and yours: It's human. Sometimes they do good and sometimes they don't. Solomon says not to invest your energy in criticizing human corruption. Instead, recognize it's going to happen and do what you can to fix it. As bad as government can be, it is better than lawlessness. Bad government is better than no government. We should try to make it better, but we should not pin any of our hopes on it. It is a flawed, human institution.

Don't Believe the Lie About Riches (5:10–20)

Our temptation, when problems arise, is to think that a little more money would solve the problem. Or maybe it would have prevented it altogether. Solomon warns us against such illogical thinking by giving us five things we should know about money.

Five Things You Should Know About Money (5:10–17)

This is a profound and practical commentary on money and financial integrity, tucked away in an Old Testament book that few Christians have read.

1. The more you have, the more you want (5:10).

   "He who loves silver will not be satisfied with silver," Solomon says. If you think really wealthy people are not trying to accumulate even more, you are wrong. Once the richest man in America, when John D. Rockefeller was asked how much money is enough, he replied, "Just a little bit more." Jesus warned against making greed and covetousness the core of one's life (Luke 12:15).

2. The more you have, the more you spend (5:11).

   "When goods increase, they increase who eat them," is Solomon's warning. This is like the law that says, "Expenses rise to meet available income." And it's true! It's almost impossible for the average American to put the brakes on his cost of living. When a salary raise comes along, up goes the lifestyle and related expenses. In *Changing The Wind*, William McDonald wrote, "When a man's possessions increase, it seems there's a corresponding increase in the number of parasites who live off him: *management consultants, tax advisers, accountants, lawyers, household employees, and sponging relatives.*"

3. The more you have, the more you worry (5:12).

   "The abundance of the rich will not permit him to sleep," Solomon wrote. When the wild fires came near our house, we were ordered to grab our valuables and evacuate. Driving away from the house, I told my wife, "It only took ten minutes to grab what is really valuable to us." Most of what every family has is "stuff" that is not worth losing a night's sleep over. When the aforementioned Rockefeller was the world's only billionaire at age 53, he worried so much about his money that his health deteriorated dramatically. He lived on crackers and milk. When he learned to give money away, his health changed; and he lived until he was 98 years old. Money is not worth losing your health over.

4. The more you have, the more you lose (5:13–14a).

   "Riches . . . perish through misfortune," warned Solomon. When the wildfires struck, the more people had, the more they lost in the fires. We're setting ourselves up for heartache by collecting "stuff." The more we have, the more we have to lose.

5. The more you have, the more you leave (5:14b–17).

   "As he came from his mother's womb, naked shall he return," is Solomon's final warning. When a rich man died, someone asked, "How much did he leave?" The answer is, "All of it." The more you accumulate in your lifetime, the more you are going to leave for others who contributed nothing to earning it. There's nothing wrong with leaving an inheritance. There is just a great irony in spending a lifetime building wealth and then handing it over to others in the end.

Let's be clear: There's nothing wrong with having money, but there is something seriously wrong with putting your hope in money.

Two Things You Need to Know About God (5:18–20)

We conclude this section with learning about two gifts God has given which deserve our gratitude.

1. Your ability to earn money is a gift from God (5:18).

   There are no "self-made men" in this world. Every person who has ever earned money has done so because of the abilities given to him by God. Solomon does not say we shouldn't be interested in earning money, having money, or living well. We just need to remember that it is God who gives the ability to earn money and prosper, and to Him should flow our gratitude. When our nation goes through down times economically, every person with a job is thankful for it. That should be our attitude all the time. It is our heritage from God (gift from Him) to "enjoy the good of all [our] labor in which [we] toil."

2. Your ability to enjoy money is a gift from God (5:19–20).

   "As for every man to whom God has given riches and wealth, and given him power to eat of it, to receive his heritage and rejoice in his labor—this is the gift of God" (verse 19). Our enjoyment of what God has provided is also "the gift of God." Have you considered that before? Have you stopped to thank God for the joy you share with friends and family when the money you have earned makes possible an enjoyable evening or a weekend trip or a summer vacation? We work and sweat and toil for what we have, forgetting that it is all the gift of God to us. There is nothing wrong with hard work (Genesis 3:17–19), but there is something wrong with anxiety about work and its results.

If we would just faithfully open our hands and thank God for the ability to work and thank God for the grace to enjoy both our work and the fruit of our labor, we would be more blessed. Putting Him first, in our work and in the enjoyment of its rewards, is the key.

Remember: Don't blame God, don't bribe God, don't be surprised at the government's failures, and don't believe the lie about riches. When troubles come, keep your eyes on Him and thank Him for it all; and you'll be glad you did.

Keep your eyes upon Jesus
Look full in His wonderful face
And the things of earth will grow strangely dim
In the light of His glory and grace!!

APPLICATION

1. What is the general guideline concerning speech given in James 1:19–20?

   a. Why is it dangerous to be swift to speak?

   b. What are the advantages of being "swift to hear"?

   c. What is the connection between being "slow to speak" and "slow to wrath"?

   d. Why is wrath so often first manifested through speech?

   e. Grade yourself on a scale of 1 to 10 (1 = slow to speak, 10 = swift to speak).

   f. Is your score a reflection of your personality or of a conscious effort to change?

2. Review the story of Job in Job 1:1–2:10.

   a. What did Job lose? (verses 1:13–19)

   b. What was Job's initial response? (verse 1:21)

   c. What does verse 1:22 say about who Job blamed for his losses?

   d. What did Job lose next? (verse 2:7)

e. What did Job's wife encourage him to do? (verse 2:9)

f. And how did Job respond? (verse 2:10)

g. Has there been a time when you've been tempted to blame God for something difficult in your life? What was your reasoning? How did you resolve the issue?

3. Read Romans 9:14–21.

   a. What is the context of this discussion? (verses 14)

   b. What is the essence of Paul's teaching? (verse 18)

   c. What objection do some raise against God's sovereign choices? (verse 19)

   d. And what is Paul's answer? Why is blaming God unacceptable? (verses 20–21)

   e. What is at the center of God's actions? (verse 17)

4. What do you learn about guarding your speech from the following verses?

   a. Psalm 39:1

   b. Proverbs 10:19

c. Proverbs 13:3

d. Isaiah 53:7

5. Read Romans 13:1–7.

   a. Who establishes civil governing authorities? (verse 1)

   b. If we criticize the government, who else are we criticizing? (verse 2)

   c. What are the two reasons for submitting to government? (verse 5)

   d. What is the only exception to submission to the government? (Acts 4:19; 5:29)

DID YOU KNOW?

In the Old Testament, a voluntary vow was a promise to God by an individual to perform some service in return for God's acting for the benefit of the one making the vow. For instance, Jacob made a vow to tithe to God of His possessions and make Bethel a memorial to God in return for God's protection and provision on a journey (Genesis 28:20–22). Vows were always voluntary, but once made, they were binding (Deuteronomy 23:21–23; Judges 11:35; Psalm 66:13). Once a vow was spoken verbally, it was binding (Deuteronomy 23:23); but vows could be redeemed at a price set by a priest. Fathers could veto daughters' and wives' vows; but if a husband let a wife's vow stand and then caused her to break it, the fault was his, not hers. Jesus warned against the abuse of vows (Matthew 5:33–37) as did James (5:12).

Note:

1. William McDonald, *Changing the Wind,* (Chicago: Moody Press, 1975) p. 47.

THE CUL-DE-SACS OF LIFE

Ecclesiastes 6:1–12

In this lesson we discover the places where we'll never find ultimate joy and meaning in life.

OUTLINE

In our world it is easy to think vocation, success, education, or advancement will bring ultimate fulfillment. Solomon counters that idea by reminding us that this world is based on God's designs. While achievement is not inherently wrong, it can never ultimately satisfy.

I. Your Money Won't Bring Meaning to Your Life
   A. Solomon's Insights
   B. Solomon's Illustrations

II. You Won't Find Joy in Your Job
   A. Your Job Can't Satisfy Your Soul
   B. Your Mind Can't Replace Your Heart
   C. Your Dreams Can't Replace Reality

III. You Won't Find Answers With Your Arguments
   A. God Has Ordained Life as He Desires It to Be
   B. Arguing With God Is an Exercise in Futility
   C. God Is Willing to Bring Meaning to Your Life
   D. God Alone Is in Charge of Your Future

OVERVIEW

People who win the lottery often wish they hadn't. Rosa Gayson of Washington won $400 a week for the rest of her life and ended up hiding in her apartment from all the people who wanted money. The whole McGugart family of New York won the Irish Sweepstakes when the father divided his millions with his sons. A year later, family members weren't speaking to each other. "It's the devil's own money," the mother concluded.

In the last lesson, we learned five important things about money and two important things about God. In Ecclesiastes 6:1–12 Solomon continues his discussion about money, but in a negative way: What happens if we try to earn and enjoy money apart from God.

YOUR MONEY WON'T BRING MEANING TO YOUR LIFE (6:1–6)

A cul-de-sac is a dead-end street and there are three of them Solomon wants us to avoid. First: Money is not a source of meaning in life.

Solomon's Insights (6:1–2)

Most Bible scholars believe Solomon is talking about himself in these first two verses, looking back on his own life. Being the wealthiest man on earth at the time in which he lived, he was qualified to say what one could and could not accomplish with money.

How did Solomon become so wealthy? The blessing of God. When he was 20 years old, the Lord appeared to him and offered him anything he might desire as the next king over Israel. Out of all the things Solomon might have asked for (what would you have requested?), Solomon asked for wisdom to judge and govern the people of Israel. Here is God's response to Solomon's request:

"Because this was in your heart, and you have not asked riches or wealth or honor or the life of your enemies, nor have you asked long life—but have asked wisdom and knowledge for yourself, that you may judge My people over whom I have made you king—wisdom and knowledge *are* granted to you; and I will give you riches and wealth and honor, such as none of the kings have had who *were* before you, nor shall any after you have the like" (2 Chronicles 1:11–12).

Solomon got what he asked for and more. That's how he became the wealthiest man in the world.

Solomon started out using his wealth wisely, building God a beautiful temple in Jerusalem. But soon his materialism gave him access to people of other cultures, and he took foreign wives and concubines—hundreds of them (1 Kings 11:3). Solomon allowed them to integrate their idolatry into the religion of Israel, and his heart was drawn away from God. This is possibly the experience Solomon is recollecting in Ecclesiastes 6:1–2.

In Ecclesiastes 5:19 Solomon wrote that money and the ability to enjoy it are gifts of God. That means the ability to use what you earn in meaningful ways in your life, not in wasteful or profligate ways, is a gift from God. When God is at the center of your life, He gives you the ability to use what He has given you in appropriate ways. When God was pushed to the side of Solomon's life, he started using his riches in self-serving ways.

Warren Wiersbe has written: "To enjoy the gifts without the Giver is idolatry, and this can never satisfy the human heart. Enjoyment without God is merely entertainment, and it doesn't satisfy. But enjoyment with God is enrichment and it brings true joy and satisfaction."

Solomon's Illustrations (6:3–6)

Though Solomon touches on the issues of wealth and money several times in Ecclesiastes, the two illustrations in these verses are without equal in making his point that meaning is not to be found in money. His illustrations are at opposite extremes, one involving a man who lives 2,000 years and has a hundred children, the other involving a child who dies at birth.

In the first illustration, Solomon employs hyperbole—exaggeration—to make his point. Methuselah is the oldest person recorded in the Bible, living 969 years. So Solomon pictures someone living twice that long (verse 6). Rehoboam, Solomon's son, had 88 children (2 Chronicles 11:21), but no one in the Bible had 100. Solomon is emphasizing the two things that indicated God's blessing in Judaism: years of life and large numbers of offspring.

But note what Solomon says about this apparently blessed man: "Indeed he has no burial" (verse 3). For a Jewish person not to have a well-attended and honorific burial was a great sign of disrespect (see the case of Jehoiakim; Jeremiah 22:18 ff.). So this man with plenty of money, a long life, and scores of children is disrespected at the end of his life. His money and his position apparently got him nothing at the end of his life because not even his children showed up to bury him. His money and prestige failed to deliver.

At the other end of the spectrum, a stillborn baby never sees the light of day: "It comes in vanity and departs in darkness, and its name is covered with darkness" (verse 4). Yet this baby, and the prosperous man who lived 2,000 years both end up in the grave. "All go to one place: all are from the dust, and all return to dust" (Ecclesiastes 3:20).

Here is the very serious point Solomon is making with these illustrations: Living without God and without meaning in life is worse than never having been born at all. To get to the end of life without meaning and honor and respect, but with a lot of money, is worse than never having lived. This is a powerful conclusion Solomon comes to, one I hope you won't miss.

But don't misinterpret what he's saying. He's not saying it's wrong to be wealthy or to live a long and prosperous life. He is saying those things can't keep you from the grave; and if you get to the grave without God, you will have lived a meaningless life. Only God brings meaning to prosperity.

You Won't Find Joy in Your Job (6:7–9)

The second way to get stuck in a dead end in life is to attach ultimate satisfaction to your job. Solomon isn't suggesting there is *no* satisfaction in work. Hopefully everyone enjoys the work they do. But to expect it to fulfill the ultimate part of your life is to ask more than it can deliver.

Your Job Can't Satisfy Your Soul (6:7)

Eugene Peterson, in *The Message*, translates this verse as, "We work to feed our appetites; meanwhile our souls go hungry." I see this everywhere in our culture as I'm sure you do.

Everyone has to work hard, even go through stretches of long hours at the job. But if your job begins to dominate your life, you will go spiritually hungry. The message of Ecclesiastes is that God has hardwired mankind to be satisfied ultimately and only by Himself. If we look for satisfaction elsewhere, such as in our vocation, we will not find it.

When one of my little grandsons came to stay at our house for the day recently, my wife got a small game device that plugged into the TV for him to use. When it wouldn't work, she asked me to take a look. While everything on the outside was in order—cables connected, switches turned "On"—it was lifeless.

I discovered that the batteries it needed were missing. As soon as we added power on the inside, it worked fine.

Life is often like that little game. We act like everything is okay, and on the outside everything is. We're plugged in, we're turned "On"—but because that God-shaped part of our life is filled with work or money or some other false filler, there's no power. Building a great and rewarding career without God in the middle of it is dangerous work. It can even be true in the ministry. We can leave God out of building a huge church as easily as building a huge company.

Your Mind Can't Replace Your Heart (6:8)

Education falls into the same category. The greatest education, devoid of God, leaves us on the same level as a fool. When the wise man and the fool stand before God, He isn't going to inquire about education or wealth or status or the things we think are so important. He's only going to care about whether we know Him. So don't let your mind replace your heart.

Your Dreams Can't Replace Reality (6:9)

Verse nine is Solomon's version of "better is a bird in the hand than two in the bush." Dreaming is good until it separates us from reality, and we start living in a fantasy world. The person who lives in the future never gets around to enjoying today. Everything is always being put off until we get more money, more time, more education. When people like this finally get it all together, they find they've missed the best years of their life.

All the way through this book, Solomon tells us to enjoy the life that God has given; and do it today. Don't let fantasies about the future keep you from experiencing the reality of today. Solomon may have glimpsed a measure of how to do this from his father, king David. In David's Psalm 16, he concluded, "You will show me the path of life; in Your presence is fullness of joy; at Your right hand are pleasures forevermore" (verse 11).

David understood what it means to find pleasure in the person of God.

You Won't Find Answers With Your Arguments (6:10–12)

Solomon anticipated that there would be arguments about this idea that life is meaningless without God. Therefore, he gives us four truths about life and God that suggest it is vain to argue with God.

God Has Ordained Life as He Desires It to Be (6:10a)

Riches and vocation and education all fail to bring happiness because of the ordinances of God. God dictates the incapacity of worldly things to bring meaning and enjoyment to our life. Could He have designed the world so that ultimate fulfillment came from accumulating money? Yes, He could have. He could have designed the world so that workaholism was the key to happiness . . . or education . . . or power and prestige. But He chose not to do that. He designed a world that needs work, money, and education but which is not dependent on them for meaning. That's just the way this God-designed world works.

Arguing With God Is an Exercise in Futility (6:10b)

Solomon says we can't contend with "Him who is mightier than [we]." It's foolish and fruitless to contend with God about the meaning of life. Paul says in Romans 9:21, "Does not the potter have power over the clay?" And the answer is "Yes." He's the Creator and we are the creatures. It is entirely inappropriate for us to raise ourselves up against God and challenge that which He has decided to do. Jesus said that life from God is meant to be abundant (John 10:10b), but that abundance must be enjoyed on His terms.

God Is Willing to Bring Meaning to Your Life (6:12)

A rhetorical question in verse 12a has an obvious answer: Only God knows what is best for man "all the days of his vain life which he passes like a shadow." And to find out what is best for your life, you have to get in touch with God. You won't find what is best for you at work, at the bank, or at the university. You'll only find it in God.

God Alone Is in Charge of Your Future (6:12)

The last rhetorical question has the same obvious answer: God. Only God knows "what will happen" in anyone's life. That's why He is worthy to be trusted. He sees around all the corners that are just blind turns to us.

Solomon's strategy in this last section is so very logical. He says life is like it is because God created it that way. Don't waste your time arguing with Him because you won't win. He's God and we're not. If you want meaning in life, go to God. If you want security for the future, go to God. Do you want to pursue your career? Try to do well for your family? Get an advanced degree? Fine—no problem. God is for all those things as long as you keep Him in the center of your world.

A man who lost everything in the recent wildfires in our area told me they were given only a few minutes to collect things from their house before fleeing. He's an engineer, so he grabbed a couple of engineering books. And he grabbed His Bible and a devotional book he was reading. The books he rescued represent the priority and balance Solomon is looking for in life. Work, vocation, education, and God in the midst of everything.

Keep that balance yourself and you'll always find the true meaning of life.

APPLICATION

1. Read Psalm 127.

   a. How is verse 1 resonant of the themes you are learning from Ecclesiastes?

   b. Is it necessary for builders to build and watchmen to watch? What does the Lord's presence add?

   c. Why is it vanity to do the things described in verse 2?

   d. Do you take advantage of the gift of sleep? (verse 2)

   e. What does "heritage" mean in verse 3?

   f. What is God rewarding with the gift of children? (verse 3)

   g. How are the children of one's youth like "arrows in the hand of a warrior?" (verse 4)

   h. What were arrows used for in Old Testament times?

   i. Why is a man (or parents) blessed when he has a quiver full of arrows (children)?

j. How would you translate the second half of verse 5 into modern terminology?

k. What is the average number of children in the families with whom you are close?

l. Why don't more Christian families strive to have a "quiver full of arrows?"

m. Given the blessings ascribed to children in this psalm, what shame might there be if those children did not return to honor their father at his death?

n. Look in the superscription (title) of this psalm and discover who the author is. How parallel is this psalm to Ecclesiastes?

2. What do the following two proverbs say about the person who lives in a fantasy world instead of the real world?

   a. Proverbs 12:11

   b. Proverbs 28:19

3. Read James 4:13–17.
   a. What were the people planning on doing as described in verse 13 ?

   b. Is there any criticism of their plans, goals, and desires?

   c. What is the criticism that is levied against them? (verses 14–15)

   d. How is this message consistent with what you are learning from Ecclesiastes?

DID YOU KNOW?

As testimony to the importance of burial as an act of honor and reverence in the Old Testament, we may cite the burials of Jacob, Joseph, Moses, and others. When Jacob was dying in Egypt, he made his sons promise to bury his body in Canaan where his grandfather, Abraham (and Sarah), and his father, Isaac (and Rebekah), and his own wife, Leah, were buried. Pharaoh granted the sons of Jacob permission to leave Egypt and bury Jacob in Canaan. All of Egypt mourned for 70 days at the passing of the Hebrew patriarch. The journey to Canaan to bury Jacob included not only all his sons and their families but dignitaries and officials from Pharaoh's court. "It was a very great gathering"—a sign of the respect accorded a man rich in years, children, and reputation.

WHEN BAD IS BETTER

Ecclesiastes 7:1–10

In this lesson we learn some of the paradoxes of walking with God.

OUTLINE

Christians believe things the world finds foolish: Give to receive, die to live, and be humble to be exalted. They seem to be the opposite of the world's way—and they are. Solomon outlines more paradoxes that, while apparently frustrating on the surface, become fruitful in the spirit.

I. **Sorrow Is Better Than Laughter**
   A. Looking Back Is Better Than Looking Forward
   B. Learning From Mourning Is Easier Than Learning From Feasting

II. **Rebuke Is Better Than Praise**

III. **The Hard Way Is Better Than the Easy Way**

IV. **Today Is Better Than Yesterday**

OVERVIEW

Consider your answers to the following statements:

I like laughter better than crying.
I like weddings better than funerals.
I like to think of my birthday better than I like to think of my dying day.
I like compliments better than criticisms.
I like the shortcut better than the long way around.
I like the good old days better than the way things are now.

Most people would agree with these declarative statements. If you do, you flunk the test that Solomon suggests in Ecclesiastes 7:1–10! It's not an actual test, of course, but one we might devise, based on the principles Solomon communicates in this section of his book.

Here's the key to what he teaches: The word "better" is found 11 times in Ecclesiastes, chapter seven. He is not teaching about things that are right and wrong in life as much as things that are better than other things—"better" meaning more depth of wisdom. Things that we often consider to be undesirable, Solomon says are often better than the alternative. Difficulties, the hard road, death, mourning—life with these experiences is better than a life without them.

Intrigued? Then study the four categories of better things in Ecclesiastes 7:1–10.

Sorrow Is Better Than Laughter (7:1–4)

According to Solomon, sorrow is better than laughter in two ways.

Looking Back Is Better Than Looking Forward (7:1)

It's hard to imagine at first how the day of one's death could be better than the day of one's birth. Solomon is not a dark, morose figure who looks on the dark side of life. He repeatedly tells us in this book that we are to enjoy life as a gift of God in light of the uncertainty life brings. He also wrote that there is a time to laugh and dance (Ecclesiastes 3:4). And 30 times in Proverbs, Solomon tells us to enjoy life (see 15:13, 15; 17:22).

To celebrate the value of laughter, Turning Point ministry put together a CD of clips of all the jokes and funny stories I've told or quoted in the pulpit during the last 20 years. It's been a popular item, even in hospitals, where one nurse uses it to lift the spirits of cancer patients. That ministry tool is right in line with the spirit of Solomon who believed in enjoying life.

So why does he say that the death day is better than the birthday? We have to go back to verse one: "A good name is better than precious ointment." In the Hebrew language, this statement contains a play on words. The Hebrew word for "name" is *shem*, and Hebrew for "ointment" is *shemen*. So Solomon is saying a good *shem* is better than a precious *shemen*. It's a literary device to catch the attention of the reader.

Here's his point: There are two days in life when a person's name is prominent—birthday and death day. What happens between those two days determines whether your name is a precious *shemen* or a foul stench. If you die with a good name, your name can never be tarnished again. But when you're born, you have an entire life ahead of you in which the possibility exists for tarnishing your name. Looking back on a good name (a good life) is better than looking forward to an unknown name (an unproved life). Therefore, the day of one's death is better than the day of one's birth. And in that sense, the sorrow of the death day is better than the laughter of the birthday.

Learning From Mourning Is Easier Than Learning From Feasting (7:2–4)

Solomon moves now to the heart—what it takes to cause us to learn and become wise. In short, we learn more from adversity than we do from prosperity. Wisdom is forged in the fire of mourning and trouble and difficulty, while fools live in the house of continual mirth.

A person who laughs all the time is denying reality, for life is not a party. There are plenty of times to laugh and rejoice, but there are also many times to mourn and weep. I know the deepest growth in my life has occurred during the ten years in which cancer has been a part of my vocabulary. I couldn't have learned what God taught me any other way. A. W. Tozer said, "God cannot use a man until he has hurt him deeply." Great men and great women are shaped by pain.

We recently had the funeral service in our church for a godly man who had been instrumental in the history of our church and schools. He had lived a godly life, established a good name, and the funeral was a celebration of his life. That's what Solomon is saying when he says the day of death is better than the day of birth, that mourning teaches us more than mirth. When a baby is born, we pray it will live a good and godly life; but we don't know. There are no guarantees. But when a person reaches the end of life and can look back on goodness and godliness, then that day of mourning is better than the rejoicing at his birth day.

Man's highest purpose is not to be happy, but to know God. And we know God the best when we face things we can't do without Him. Our church saw a number of people come to know Christ through the tragedy surrounding the wild fires in our area. Troubles cause all of us to stop the routine and ask more serious questions about life. For that reason, sorrow is better than laughter.

Rebuke Is Better Than Praise (7:5–6)

Are you beginning to sense why the answers to Solomon's quiz are the opposite of what we might expect? If so, then you'll not be surprised to learn that rebuke is better than praise.

We normally resist the pain of a rebuke, but Solomon says rebuke from a wise man is far better than the songs of fools. He likens the praise of a fool to the crackling of thorns in a fire. This is an illustration from life in biblical days. When a short burst of heat was needed in a fire, branches from a thorny plant would be thrown on the fire because they flamed up so quickly and intensely. But thorns would never be used for a fire you wanted to last a long time. Likewise, the praise of fools is intense, but temporary; whereas the rebuke of a wise man has long-lasting benefit.

Accepting rebuke is a sign of wisdom which Solomon mentions throughout his writings (Proverbs 10:17; 12:1; 15:5; 17:10; 25:12; 27:5; 29:1). But we would much rather hear the words of a "stroker"—someone who strokes us and makes us feel good about ourselves. But a "stroker" can't be trusted! They usually have ulterior motives for why they're pumping us up—probably to curry our favor down the road. They "stroke" us and then they strike; a friend becomes an enemy.

Solomon says to be more interested in the rebuke of someone who is wise, a person who loves you, than the songs and strokes of a person who is insincere. If you practice this principle for a lifetime, you will reap the permanent benefits of wisdom and avoid the downfalls of flattery.

The Hard Way Is Better Than the Easy Way (7:7–9)

I recently set out to attend one of our school's "away" basketball games. I knew how to get to the other school but decided to take a shortcut and got so lost even the navigation computer in my car couldn't figure out where I was. After wandering around aimlessly I ended up back home, never having seen the game. Solomon says the long way is better than the short way.

A bribe is a shortcut—trying to make something happen faster than it otherwise would (verse 7). But why is the end of a thing better than the beginning? Because we ought to be focusing on where we are headed before we begin the journey. What will be the results of my actions, the outcome of my deeds?

Satan always puts his best up front, while God saves His best for last. The immediate and initial impact of alcohol, drugs, or illicit sex may be exciting on the front end, but the backside of those actions is destruction. That's why the end is better than the beginning. A person who ends well did so because he made wise choices on the front end.

I often hear people say that the first days and years of marriage are the best. No they're not! They are the noisiest and most tumultuous by far as two people try to blend their lives together. The best days of a marriage are (or should be) the latter days. Two people spend their adult years together and love each other in spite of everything that comes. The best years of marriage are the latter years. The end of a thing is better than the beginning.

Today Is Better Than Yesterday (7:10)

Almost everyone longs for "the good old days." But "the good old days" are a myth; they don't exist. Think about it: The days we live in right now will be "the good old days" of the future. Somehow these days will look better 30 years from now.

Solomon says, "Do not say, 'Why were the former days better than these?'" In truth, he means, they weren't. He warns us not to live our lives in the past. Those days appear good only to those who are trying to avoid living in the present.

All of these paradoxes that Solomon is expressing have been summarized beautifully in a poem called "The Valley of Vision:"

Lord, high and holy, meek and lowly,
Thou hast brought me to the valley of vision,

Where I live in the depths but see thee in the heights;
Hemmed in by mountains of sin I behold thy glory.

Let me learn by paradox
That the way down is the way up
That to be low is to be high
That the broken heart is the healed heart,
That the contrite spirit is the rejoicing spirit,
That the repenting soul is the victorious soul,
That to have nothing is to possess all,
That to bear the cross is to wear the crown,
That to give is to receive,
That the valley is the place of vision.

Lord, in the daytime stars can be seen from the deepest wells,
And the deeper the wells the brighter thy stars shine;
Let me find thy light in my darkness,
Thy life in my death,
Thy joy in my sorrow,
Thy grace in my sin,
Thy riches in my poverty
Thy glory in my valley.
[from *The Valley of Vision, A Collection of Puritan Prayers and Devotions,* Arthur Bennett, Editor, 1975]

The glory of God is found in the valley, not on the mountaintop. When we're in the valley, we are forced to look up and see God "high and lifted up" (Isaiah 6:1).

If you are not sure how God uses these paradoxical situations, let me remind you of the truth of Romans 8:28: "And we know that all things work together for good to those who love God, to those who are the called according to His purpose." That's how He does it. He takes things that look like they are the opposite of good and causes them to work together for good and His glory. The world would say that the easy way is better than the hard way; but when God gets through rearranging things for His children, the hard way always turns out to be better.

Life can be confusing at present (Romans 8:22). But in the midst of that confusion, God's Holy Spirit comes to our aid and "helps in our weaknesses" by making intercession for us right in the midst of difficult circumstances (Romans 8:26). God then uses those prayers to cause all things to work together for good.

We've already learned in Ecclesiastes that God's plan is good, His purpose is clear, and His program is mysterious. That's why we don't always know how to pray. That fact doesn't change the goodness or clarity of God's plan or purpose. It does, however, change the way we pray and depend on the Lord. We have to trust Him for what is mysterious to us but clear to Him. We pray and we groan in our spirit, and the Spirit makes intercession for us according to the mysteries of the will of God. I stop and remember that what I know about God is far more important than what I can't figure out.

This is the Christian life, my friend. We live in the midst of paradoxes which the world finds foolish, but which we find fruitful. As the old gospel song says, "We'll understand it better by and by." Take Solomon's test again, and see if his answers make more sense in light of Ecclesiastes, chapter three.

APPLICATION

1. What do you learn about the enjoyment of life (and the opposite) from the following verses in Proverbs?

   a. 12:25

   b. 14:30

   c. 15:13

   d. 15:15

   e. 15:30

   f. 17:22

   g. 18:14

2. What do you learn about the value of affliction from these verses in Psalm 119?

   a. verse 67

   b. verse 71–72

   c. verse 74

   d. verse 75

3. Describe a time of affliction you have been through recently and what you learned from it:

   a. When it began, was your first thought "this is a good thing" or "this is a bad thing"?

   b. What was your concluding thought?

4. Read 2 Timothy 3:16–17.

   a. List the four purposes and benefits of the Word of God:

      1.

      2.

      3.

      4.

   b. What significance do you attach to the fact that the purposes are evenly divided between instruction (doctrine, righteousness) and correction (reproof, correction)?

   c. What is an area of your life in which the Bible provided significant correction to your previous behavior?

   d. What benefit can you attach to the correction you received?

   e. How readily did you take to the correction?

5. What happens to the person who fails to receive correction? (Proverbs 10:17)

   a. What is the person who hates correction? (Proverbs 12:1)

   b. What does a fool do? (Proverbs 15:5)

c. What is the value of rebuke that is given and received? (Proverbs 25:12)

d. What is better than concealed love? (Proverbs 27:5)

e. What happens to a stiff-necked person? (Proverbs 29:1)

6. Read Matthew 17:1–9.

a. What did Peter, James, and John witness? (verse 2)

b. Where did this take place? (verse 1)

c. Where did Peter want to stay? (verse 4)

d. Where did Jesus lead them when they were finished? (verse 9)

e. What implications do you draw from this event, location, and re-location?

DID YOU KNOW?

The *American Heritage Dictionary* says a paradox is "a seemingly contradictory statement that may nonetheless be true," or "a statement contrary to received opinion." Some of the message of the Bible seems either contradictory or contrary to received opinion. The word comes from Greek *paradoxos,* "conflicting with expectation" (*para,* beyond, plus *doxa,* opinion; beyond, or against, prevailing opinion). Believing that life comes through dying, or that we receive by giving, appears contradictory. But that's because we're used to the world's way of interpreting reality. Exact truth is found in the kingdom of God regardless of how it appears in the world.

WISDOM TO BE THANKFUL FOR

Ecclesiastes 7:11–29

In this lesson we discover two benefits of wisdom: perspective on life and power for living.

OUTLINE

Life is a puzzle—a process of making disjointed pieces fit together into a big picture. When we know what to do, we lack power. And when we feel empowered, sometimes we don't know what to do. Wisdom is the skill of living—the ability to know what to do and have strength to do it.

I. Thank God for the Perspective of Wisdom

A. Wisdom to Deal With Prosperity

B. Wisdom to Deal With Providence

C. Wisdom to Deal With the Puzzles of Life

II. Thank God for the Power of Wisdom

A. Wisdom to Deal With the Problems We Encounter

B. Wisdom to Deal With the People We Employ

C. Wisdom to Deal With the Perplexities We Experience

D. Wisdom to Deal With the Pitfalls We Escape

OVERVIEW

Max Lucado tells a wonderful story about a poor woodcutter who possessed the essence of true wisdom.

The woodcutter, though poor, was the envy of his village because he owned a beautiful white horse. Many people offered to buy the steed, but the woodcutter refused. One morning the woodcutter awoke to find his prize horse was gone. The villagers laughed at him, saying he should have sold him while he had the chance—at least he would have the money. Now the woodcutter had nothing.

But the woodcutter cautioned the villagers not to judge too quickly regarding the horse's disappearance. He reminded them that all they knew was that the horse was gone. They didn't know whether that would be a blessing or a curse. The villagers thought the old man was a fool.

But 15 days later the horse returned, bringing a dozen wild horses with him. The villagers confessed they had been wrong. But again the woodcutter cautioned them not to go too far. All they knew was that the horse was back with a dozen more. Whether that was a blessing or a curse only time would tell. They shouldn't judge so much based on so little information. "I am content with what I know. I am not perturbed by what I don't," he said.

The man's son set out to break and train the wild horses, but one day he fell from one of the horses and broke both legs. The villagers were quick to judge that the return of the white horse with the others had, indeed, been a curse. The old man's only helper was now helpless. Yes, the horses were a curse.

Again the old man cautioned them against their judging. All we know, he said, is that my son has broken his legs. More than that we cannot say. "We only have a fragment. Life comes in fragments."

Soon the country engaged in a war and all the village's young men were required to join the army. Only the woodcutter's son was exempted because of his broken legs. The villagers wailed over the conscription of their sons and agreed that, surely, the horses, and the son's broken legs, had been a blessing. The son had been saved from going to war.

Exasperated with the villagers, the woodcutter said, "It is impossible to talk with you. You always draw conclusions. No one knows if it is a blessing or a curse. No one is wise enough to know. Only God knows." (adapted from Max Lucado, *The Eye of the Storm*)

The woodcutter captured perfectly the message in this portion of Ecclesiastes, chapter seven. Solomon is going to convey that wisdom is found in not trying to know what you cannot know. Or, to say it differently, wisdom is found in being content with what you can know. Only God has the entire manuscript; we have only a page here and there.

Wisdom can be a practical and powerful influence in our lives if we let it, delivering us from all manner of worry and discontent. To that end, Solomon says we should thank God for the perspective and the power of wisdom.

Thank God for the Perspective of Wisdom (7:11–18)

Wisdom may not solve all of our problems or smooth out all of our rough roads, but it can give us perspective.

Wisdom to Deal With Prosperity (7:11–12)

It is better to have wisdom than a great fortune or grand inheritance. Wisdom is not subject to the fluctuations in the economy. If you have wisdom and wealth, you are doubly blessed, Solomon says. Solomon wrote in Proverbs that to find wisdom is to find life and obtain favor from God (8:35).

Wisdom is like a shelter, a stronger fortress than money. It's interesting how few people we see who possess both wisdom and wealth. Wealth without wisdom can result in misery; wisdom can give perspective on the right use of wealth. One is actually better off poor than to have wealth with no wisdom.

Wisdom to Deal With Providence (7:13–14)

Solomon says to consider the work of God: Who can straighten out the things He makes crooked (verse 13)? We would like to straighten out the afflictions we find ourselves in, but we can't. It's good to know God is with us in the crooked places in life; but given the choice, we'd just as soon not go through them. We'd like to straighten every crooked thing.

Walter Kaiser, an Old Testament scholar, has rendered these verses this way:

> Look with wonder, admire, and silently wait for the result of God's work! The contrasts of life are deliberately

> allowed by God so that men should ultimately develop a simple trust and dependence in God. For prosperity and the goods from God's hand, be thankful and rejoice. But in adversity and the crookedness of life, think. Reflect on the goodness of God and the comprehensiveness of His plan for men.

It's easy to give thanks to God for the good times, but are we as quick to thank Him for what we have learned in the crooked places? Wisdom can help us be consistent in dealing with Providence.

When Job lost everything he had in one fell swoop, then lost his health as well, his wife encouraged him to curse God. He responded, "Shall we indeed accept good from God, and shall we not accept adversity?" (Job 2:10) Now that's wisdom! Job had perspective on Providence. He didn't curse God. Instead, he dealt with what he knew, not what he didn't know.

Warren Wiersbe wrote this about wisdom on God's dealing with us:

> God balances our lives by giving us enough blessings to keep us happy and enough burdens to keep us humble. If all we had were blessings in our hands, we would fall right over, so the Lord balances the blessings in our hands with burdens on our backs. That helps keep us steady, and as we yield to Him, we can even turn burdens into blessings.

God balances, by His providence, the blessings and burdens that come into our lives. That balance allows us to stand up straight, bent neither forward nor backward, and continue to look to Him as we walk through this life.

Wisdom to Deal With the Puzzles of Life (7:15–18)

Your life is just as busy and complicated as mine is, so you know what I mean when I say life is a puzzle. Every day there are things we can't figure out by ourselves. We need God's wisdom daily to find the pieces for building the big picture.

1. The puzzle of reversed rewards (7:15)

   Solomon again notes the puzzle of the righteous perishing and the wicked prospering. We dealt with this in an earlier lesson, but here let's note what Solomon says later in this book: "As you do not know what is the way of the wind, or how the bones grow in the womb of her who is with child, so you do not know the works of God who makes everything" (Ecclesiastes 11:5).

We don't, and can't, know the works of God. His ways are higher than our ways, and I worship Him for that very reason. If I could figure out everything about Him, I would not be in awe of Him. If rewards are reversed now, I know that puzzle will be solved one day when God balances the scales of justice.

We see good people suffer and bad people prosper all around us today. Wisdom will not agonize over what it cannot know. Instead we commit those things to the sovereignty of God and wait for Him to conclude His purposes. God is both loving and powerful, so reversed rewards don't exist due to His impotence in some area. There is another reason: the mystery of His will and ways. Remember the woodcutter: We see only a page, a fragment, while God sees the whole story.

2. The puzzle of righteous rhetoric (7:16–18)

   Solomon's words in these three verses are among the most misunderstood in the book. Liberal interpreters believe Solomon is saying there is no need for extreme holiness, no need to be "overly righteous" (verse 16). Find the middle ground . . . live a little . . . relax and enjoy life . . . nobody's perfect. Solomon definitely says we are to enjoy life, but not at the expense of holiness.

   Mediocrity won't get us into heaven, but it will get us into hell. God doesn't grade on the curve. We don't get to heaven by being a little better than the next guy. Solomon is making the point that we are not to go around flaunting our righteousness or our humility. We are to be righteous, but not in a self-promoting way. He is not warning about being too righteous, but about righteous rhetoric that is not backed up by deeds. The way to avoid the ditch of self-righteousness and false humility is to stay in the middle: "It is good to grasp the one and not let go of the other. The man who fears God will avoid all extremes" (verse 18, NIV).

   Solomon is saying, "Don't get caught up in self-righteousness or false humility." Walk in the fear of God between the two extremes.

Thank God for the Power of Wisdom (7:19–29)

Wisdom gives perspective on God's providence, and it also gives power.

Wisdom to Deal With the Problems We Encounter (7:19–20)

The beginning of wisdom is the fear of the Lord (Proverbs 1:7; 9:10); and when we fear the Lord, we will not fear any man or "ten rulers of the city" (verse 19). There is power in not living in fear. Remember Shadrach, Meshach, and Abed-Nego in the book of Daniel? When they were threatened with death by fire, they told king Nebuchadnezzar, "Fine. We trust God. He can rescue us if it's His will. But even if He doesn't, we're not bowing down to you." There is strength in knowing God.

Wisdom to Deal With the People We Employ (7:21–22)

We cannot live on an emotional roller coaster based on what people say about us. I had to learn as the pastor of a large church that I can't take to heart every negative criticism I hear. That doesn't mean I disregard the opinions of others; it just means I don't live my life based on "public opinion polls." And you shouldn't either. Listen for God's words to you. If He says or confirms something to your heart, then wisdom will give you power to act on it.

Wisdom to Deal With the Perplexities We Experience (7:23–25)

Solomon says, "As for that which is far off and exceedingly deep, who can find it out" (verse 24)? That's wisdom talking. I remember hearing when I was a young boy, "I don't know the future, but I know who holds the future." Solomon is warning us yet again not to obsess about things we can't understand in this life. God's plan is good, His purpose is clear, but His program is mysterious. What I don't know about His program is balanced by what I know about Him: He is good. Just like you will trust a good friend to take care of something without your having to know all the details, so wisdom allows you to trust God. You know your friend's character—how much more trustworthy is the character of God?

Wisdom to Deal With the Pitfalls We Escape (7:26–29)

This last point may seem slightly out of context, but it is on target as far as a power needed today, especially by men: the power to avoid illicit relationships. Wisdom will keep us from falling into the pit of immorality and preserve us from self-induced destruction.

The late pastor Ray Stedman summarized Solomon's qualifications to insert this warning in a discussion on wisdom:

"Solomon was trapped by sexual seductions. He went looking for love. Many a man or woman can echo what he is saying. He went looking for love, and thought he would find it in a relationship with a woman. He went looking for that which would support him, strengthen him and make him feel life was worth the living, but what he found was nothing but a fleeting sexual thrill. He found himself involved with a woman who did not give him what he was looking for at all; he still felt the same empty loneliness as before."

When I read Solomon's words about the perspectives and power of wisdom, I am so thankful to be a New Testament saint. For Paul wrote in Colossians 2:3 that "in [Jesus Christ] are hidden all the treasures of wisdom and knowledge." Thankfully we don't have to have our own wisdom. We can have the wisdom of God by having Christ. Only through Him do I gain the perspective and power of God to live life wisely.

Do you have perspective and power adequate for the life you are living? If you have Christ, you do. Gaining Him is the wisest thing you will ever do.

APPLICATION

1. Read Proverbs 1:1–7.

   a. Note the reasons the book of Proverbs was compiled:

   - verse 2: to know __________ and __________.
   - verse 2: to perceive the __________ of __________.
   - verse 3: to receive the instruction of __________,

     __________, __________, and __________.
   - verse 4: to give __________ to the __________.
   - verse 4: to the young man __________ and __________.

   b. What will the wise man and man of understanding gain from Proverbs? (verse 5)

   c. How does verse 6 relate to Matthew 13:10–13? What kind of wisdom did the disciples need?

   d. Where does all knowledge and wisdom begin? (Proverbs 1:7)

   e. How would you describe "the fear of the Lord?" (verse 7)

   f. What is the source of understanding? (Proverbs 9:10b)

g. What impact on your own wisdom do you think regular reading of Proverbs would have?

2. Read Proverbs 2:1–22.

   a. What are the conditions specified in the "if" clauses in the opening verses?

      - verse 1: if you . . .

      - verse 3: if you . . .

      - verse 4: if you . . .

   b. What are the results that will come from fulfilling the conditions?

      - verse 5: then . . .

      - verses 6–8: for . . .

      - verse 9: then . . .

c. What do you think of the process of acquiring wisdom being as laborious as mining for silver? (verse 4)

d. Do you think that has anything to do with the scarcity of wisdom today?

e. Practically speaking, how would you translate verse 4 into modern application?

f. What do you think verse 3 refers to? To whom are you crying out and lifting up your voice?

g. How often do you pray for wisdom?

h. How do others react when they find someone who has true wisdom? (Psalm 119:74, 79)

DID YOU KNOW?

The root meaning of wisdom in the Old Testament is the idea of skill. That's why the Hebrew root word for wisdom (*hakam*) shows up in lots of places not seemingly connected to wisdom, but very much connected to skill. Garment makers (Exodus 28:3), craftsmen and designers (Exodus 35:35), shrewd people (2 Samuel 13:3), enchanters (Psalm 58:5), ants (Proverbs 30:24–28), idol makers (Isaiah 40:20), and seamen (Ezekiel 27:8) were all said to possess "wisdom," or skill. Therefore, applying *hakam* to life, wisdom becomes "the skill of living." As a craftsman fashions a piece of art, so we fashion a life of beauty and utility by the choices we make.

Facing Life With Humility

Ecclesiastes 8:1–17

In this lesson we learn five definitions of humility.

OUTLINE

Being self-centered creatures, there is little in life we would not change to suit ourselves if we could. But there are more things in life we can't change than those we can. And in that truth is a recipe for wisdom through humility. Humility means being content when change is impossible.

I. **Humility Is Knowing What You Don't Know**

II. **Humility Is Living With What You Don't Like**

III. **Humility Is Accepting What You Can't Change**
   - A. Death
   - B. Distress
   - C. Deception
   - D. Defiance

IV. **Humility Is Enjoying What You Can't Explain**

V. **Humility Is Discovering What You Can't Discover**

OVERVIEW

One of my favorite players in the National Football League is Kurt Werner, a wonderfully talented quarterback who led the St. Louis Rams to the Super Bowl. He was named the Most Valuable Player of the league and of the Super Bowl—and the next thing you know he was sitting on the bench, not playing. He went through a period of not doing too well, got injured; and while he was recuperating, the back-up quarterback won his job. So he went from MVP to holding a clipboard and taking notes on the sidelines. Talk about a humbling transition!

Life is a process of learning humility. Even our children keep us humble. One night my wife and I were enjoying a quiet evening at home playing one of our favorite board games. Our oldest daughter called and asked what we were doing. I told her we were playing the game. "Just the two of you? That's cute!" she said. After she hung up, I said to my wife, "I wonder what they think we do? As if, now that they're gone, we just stopped living?" Children can keep you humble.

The actor Tom Selleck wrote, "Whenever I get full of myself, I remember the nice couple who approached me with a camera on a street in Honolulu one day. When I struck a pose for them, the man said, 'No, no. We want you to take a picture of us.'" Even strangers can keep us humble.

In the eighth chapter of Ecclesiastes, Solomon reminds us about things that make us humble.

Humility Is Knowing What You Don't Know (8:1)

Throughout the Bible, we are warned against being wise in our own eyes. Solomon says that a wise man has a shining face, a glowing countenance. A wise man knows some things and some things he doesn't. But "the sternness of his face is changed" because he is not uptight about what he doesn't know. He is wise, and his wisdom makes him humble.

In 1 Corinthians 8:2, Paul wrote, "And if anyone thinks that he knows anything, he knows nothing yet as he ought to know." Knowledge is a never-ending pursuit, an exercise in humility as we discover what we don't know. Two decades ago researchers told us that the world's knowledge changed every 38 years. That is, the knowledge you could acquire in 38 years was equal to all the knowledge that existed before. Today the knowledge of the world changes every single year! Today, more knowledge is accumulated in one year than in all the years that have ever been. And it will keep growing every year.

My grandchildren understand modern electrical gadgets better than I do because they have grown up with them. Knowledge is exploding—and it's getting harder and harder to keep up. It is a wise and humble man who knows what he doesn't know, what he can't know, and what he doesn't need to know—because you can't know it all. Anyone who thinks he "knows it all" is already suffering from pride.

Humility Is Living With What You Don't Like (8:2–7)

Much of our daily lives is controlled by the dictates and desires, not to mention needs, of others—whether the government or a family member. Daily we have to remind ourselves that we'll be required to do things we'd rather not do. Solomon gives us an illustration in verses 2–7 of the fact that we all have to live with what we don't like.

Being in a situation you can't control is humbling. A citizen who is under the power and control of a king is humbled by having to obey. But Solomon says, "Keep the king's commandment for the sake of your oath to God" (verse 2)—not because you like the king. Even when you don't like what you're being made to do, do it out of loyalty to God. This is the essence of Paul's message to the church in Rome about submitting to civil authorities (Romans 13:1–2). As long as what we're being asked to do doesn't disobey the commands of God, we are to do it.

Eugene Peterson's version of Ecclesiastes 8:2–7 is very helpful:

> Do what your king commands; you gave a sacred oath of obedience. [3] Don't worryingly second-guess your orders or try to back out when the task is unpleasant. You're serving his pleasure, not yours. [4] The king has the last word. Who dares say to him, "What are you doing?" [5] Carrying out orders won't hurt you a bit; the wise person obeys promptly and accurately. [6] Yes, there's a right time and way for everything, even though, unfortunately, we miss it for the most part. [7] It's true that no one knows what's going to happen, or when. Who's around to tell us?

Humility is knowing what you don't know and living with what you don't like.

Humility Is Accepting What You Can't Change (8:8–14)

This point follows the one above: If we're doing something we don't like, we can't change it because we're not in control. It's obvious that if we could change it, we would! So much of life is uncontrollable. As soon as we think we've got a handle on things . . . they're out of control again. Solomon says there are four things you will never be able to control.

Death (8:8)

We often hear that there are two things we'll never change: death and taxes. In fact, taxes can and do change, but death doesn't. It is the great leveler, the great symbol of just how little control over "things" we actually have.

What we don't know about death is when it will find us. Solomon speaks of it in the context of war, a timely way for us to think of it with so many of our armed forces serving in high-tension points in the world. But soldiers aren't the only ones living on the edge—death can find any one of us at any time. And we cannot elude it.

There is a legend of a merchant in Baghdad who sent his servant to the market. The servant returned home, ashen and shaken. He told his master he had just encountered Death at the market and begged for use of his master's horse to flee to Samarra to hide. The merchant agreed and the servant fled. Later, when the merchant was in the market, he saw Death and asked why she had threatened his servant that morning. Death replied that she had not meant to startle the servant. She was surprised to see him in the market in Baghdad since she had an appointment to meet him that night in Samarra.

When it comes to death, "you can run, but you can't hide." Some people who can afford it are now trying to thwart death by paying large sums to have themselves, or just their heads, frozen, believing that one day science will make it possible for their lives to be returned to them. It's a waste of money, for it is appointed unto man once to die and then comes the judgment (Hebrews 9:27). Death is a reality of life that we have no control over, and wisdom embraces that fact.

Distress (8:9)

Solomon says, "There is a time in which one man rules over another to his own hurt." We will all be disappointed and hurt by others—and sometimes by those we trust the most. That's how we learn to keep our expectations focused on the Lord who never disappoints, and not on people. The wise man is one who assesses his life and decides what he can change, what hurt he can prevent, and what he can control—and what he can't. Everyone will suffer distress in this life. That's just the way it is. The answer is not vengeance—it is humility born out of wisdom.

Deception (8:10)

Solomon comments about the funeral of a man who had frequented the temple, but who had lived an ungodly life. He had deceived the people who knew him, and they eulogized him in grand fashion. All this while the godly people of the city were ignored and forgotten. "This also is vanity," Solomon says (verse 10).

This even happens today. We see on television coverage of the death of a public figure of some sort who everyone knows was a scoundrel. Yet he is heralded as a passing saint. Meanwhile, good people, doing noble work, labor in obscurity. There is a great deal of deception in this world which you and I cannot change.

Defiance (8:11–14)

Throughout all sectors of society we see people shaking their fists in the face of authorities—ultimately in the face of God. Solomon says because people do not experience judgment for their sins, they think nothing is going to happen; and they defiantly continue in their rebellious ways. What they forget is that God is the ultimate judge. Whether human authorities make them pay or not, God will. And He doesn't work on our timetable. It is humbling to have to pay a speeding ticket when people doing much worse are getting away with it. But wisdom will leave ultimate judgment to God.

Humility Is Enjoying What You Can't Explain (8:15)

The fourth characteristic of humility is enjoying what you can't explain. For the fourth time, Solomon reminds us that it is our privilege to "eat, drink, and be merry" in this life. This seems odd coming on the heels of death, distress, deception, and defiance, but that's the whole point. We can't control or change any of those things, so don't get caught up in trying to do the impossible. Focus on what you can control: the choice to enjoy the life Almighty God has given you as His gift.

God has not called us to forfeit the joy of life as a result of despondency over things we can't explain and can't change. We don't eat, drink, and pursue merriment like the world without a thought of tomorrow. We eat, drink, and pursue merriment out of gratitude to the God who gives us that privilege in the midst of a world that He controls.

As Christians, we don't sit around and mope over things we can't control and can't change. We count each day as precious and live it to its fullest, thanking God all the while for the opportunity.

Humility Is Discovering What You Can't Discover (8:16–17)

Here are Solomon's final words about humility: "Then I saw all the work of God, that a man cannot find out the work that is done under the sun. For though a man labors to discover it, yet he will not find it; moreover, though a wise man attempts to know it, he will not be able to find it."

The French philosopher Blaise Pascal wrote in his famous *Pensées* this statement. Listen carefully to what he said:

> If there were no obscurity, man would not feel his corruption; if there were no light, man could not hope for a cure. Thus it is not only right but useful for us that God should be partly concealed and partly revealed, since it is equally dangerous for man to know God without knowing his own wretchedness as to know his wretchedness without knowing God.

Did you get that? "If there were no obscurity, man would not feel his corruption." If we could know all about God and this world, we wouldn't have any sense of our own shortcomings or sinfulness. God has concealed things on purpose in order that we might know His greatness and our limitations, in order that we might be forced to seek after Him to discover what we don't know. But when we reach the limits of our discovery at any given moment, if we are humble, we will rest. We will recognize the limitations He has put in place and be willing to stop and take up the search another day. The discovery of God and His ways in this world is a never-ending quest. He is infinite and we are finite. Wisdom and humility acknowledge the gap that exists between Him and us and doesn't try to close it beyond what He allows.

Think of the gap that would exist if God had not chosen to close it as much as He did by sending His Son, Jesus Christ, into the world. He became flesh and dwelt among us, allowing us to behold the glory of God among men, full of grace and truth (John 1:14). The apostle Paul recounts in detail how Christ "made Himself of no reputation . . . and being found in appearance as a man, He humbled Himself and became obedient to the point of death, even the death of the cross" (Philippians 2:7–8).

Have you closed the gap between yourself and God, crossing over via the bridge named Jesus? Imitating the humility of Jesus is the first step in discovering God.

APPLICATION

1. Read James 4:1–6.
   a. What is the context of this passage? (verses 1–2)

   b. What is always at work when people argue? (the opposite of humility)

   c. How can a lack of humility affect our prayer life? (verse 3)

   d. How can friendship with the world reveal a lack of humility in our life? (verse 4)

   e. What is God's perspective toward the proud? (verse 6a)

   f. What does God give to the humble? (verse 6b)

   g. What does verse 6b mean in a practical way?

   h. How might grace manifest itself in the situations described in verses 1 and 2?

   i. If God resists the proud (those who fight), how might His resistance be manifested?

2. Read 1 Peter 5:1–7.

   a. What is the opening context of these verses? (verses 1–4)

   b. What kind of humility is required of younger people in the church? (verse 5a)

   c. What is required of everyone in the church, elders and younger people alike? (verse 5b)

   d. How do elders rule the church with humility?

   e. What would characterize an elder who didn't rule with humility?

   f. What warning about pride does Paul issue to elders in 1 Timothy 3:6?

   g. What does God ultimately do for the humble? (1 Peter 5:6)

   h. How would you apply verse 7 to the theme of this lesson: that there are things in life we can't control or change?

   i. What are the hardest things in your life to "cast upon Him"—things you'd like to control or change but can't?

3. We learned in this lesson not to get caught up in trying to do the impossible. What four things, according to Solomon, are impossible for us to control or change?

4. The humble and wise man assesses his life and decides:

   a. What he can ____________________,

   b. What hurt he can ________________,

   c. and what he can _________________, and what he can't.

5. Imitating the humility of Jesus is the first step in discovering God. How can we imitate Jesus' humility in our own life?

DID YOU KNOW?

Philippians 2:5–11 is one of the most important passages of theology in the New Testament, specifically the theology of the person of Christ (the doctrine of Christology). Theologians call this passage the "Kenosis" passage, referring to the Greek verb *kenoo,* "to empty." In verse 7, Paul says Christ "emptied Himself" (NASB) and took on the form of a bond servant. Discussion throughout church history has centered around this "emptying." Of what did Christ empty Himself? Deity? The right to exercise the prerogatives of Deity on earth? The NKJV translates it well: "[He] made Himself of no reputation."

The Subject Nobody Talks About

Ecclesiastes 9:1–18

In this lesson we talk biblically about what no one wants to talk about: death.

OUTLINE

When people talk about death and dying, they often use terms like passing on, slipping away, going to a better place, and enjoying rewards. Some would rather talk about the end of life in anything but realistic terms. Not Solomon. He speaks honestly—realism balanced with hope.

I. The Certainty of Death

A. The Reality of Death

B. The Responses to Death

II. The Complexity of Life

A. In This Life, the Best Man Isn't Always Rewarded

B. In This Life, a Good Man Isn't Always Remembered

OVERVIEW

A Chicago gambler named Willy Stokes, Jr., was buried in his Cadillac Seville made into a coffin. He was sitting at the steering wheel wearing a hot pink suit, hands on the wheel, with five $100 bills stuffed between his left thumb and forefinger. One of his gangland buddies walked by the coffin-car and said, "Man, that's living!"

Actually, that's dying. You can give death a hot pink suit and a fancy Cadillac, but it doesn't change a thing. Dead is dead.

Why is everyone so afraid to face the reality of death? The comedian and movie director Woody Allen once said, "I'm not afraid to die. I just don't want to be there when it happens."

Solomon has written a book filled with realism, and he is not afraid to talk about death. He has said throughout this book that if you try to live your life without God, it will be a meaningless life—and therefore a meaningless death. To get to the end of a life of emptiness and despair and face the reality of who-knows-what after death . . . that could make anyone afraid to confront the reality of dying.

This may seem like a morbid subject to some, but it is not. It is a realistic and relevant subject. In fact, nothing is more relevant to every person who reads the book, than a discussion of death. The last time I checked, the statistics on people dying were exactly 100 percent. That makes it a relevant subject.

The Certainty of Death (9:1–10)

In verses 1–10 Solomon confronts the reality of death and talks about what our response to death should be.

The Reality of Death (9:1–2)

An old Italian proverb says, "When the chess game is over, the pawns, the rooks, the kings, the queens, all go back into the same box." One thing the righteous and the wicked share in common, Solomon says, is that they both die. Life ends the same way for everyone on planet earth (Hebrews 9:27).

You would think something so pervasive would be easily discussed, but it's not. We don't even like to say the word "death." We say, "passed away," "passed on," "went to be with the Lord," "got promoted to heaven," "in a better place," and "enjoying their rest." If any of those are true, it's because something else happened first: They died!

The late pastor Ray Stedman had a thought on why people are so uncomfortable at funerals: "A funeral is one event where one can no longer escape ultimate reality. A funeral is proof that we can no longer escape ultimate reality . . . that we are not in control of our own lives." The subject of death is avoided because everyone knows it's coming—the one thing in life they can't escape.

The Responses to Death (9:3–10)

We can identity two things not to do and one thing to do when it comes to responding to death.

1. Don't deny it (9:3).

   How we respond to death says a lot about the contents of our heart—what we really believe. When I was a student in seminary, I worked as a chaplain at a major hospital for two years. I came in contact with death, and the people whose lives were affected, every day. I saw people devastated by death, and I saw people face death with calm and assurance. Death tells a lot about who we are.

   Some people choose to deny the reality of death. As a young pastor, I was asked to conduct the funeral of someone I had never met. At the service, as I was walking to my car, a young woman came running across the parking lot screaming at me, using language I hadn't heard in a long time. She was a daughter of the deceased, and was angry that I had mentioned her sister in my remarks, but had not mentioned her. Of course, not knowing the deceased, I was using information furnished to me by others and had not intentionally omitted mention of her. But she was so angry over the death of her father that she chose to vent on me.

   Denying death is a dead-end street; a strategy with nowhere to go except despair and frustration.

2. Don't ignore it (9:4–6).

   Another response to death is to hope against hope that it will pass you by. "Where there's life, there's hope," comes from verse four. "A living dog is better than a dead lion" (verse 4), this person says. Better to be a despised dog and alive, than the king of the beasts, but dead.

   The problem with this approach is that hope is only valid when it is based on reality. Hope is like faith—it all depends on the object of the hope or faith. Hope in hope avails nothing, but hope in Christ who conquered death is totally different. However, hope in Christ doesn't ignore death. It acknowledges that death is real but has been overcome by the resurrection of Christ.

Solomon reminds us of everything that can't be done after we die—especially the person who dies apart from God (verses 5–6). But there's no reason we can't do those things while we're alive. It's a reminder that death is coming—live life while we can!

3. Do embrace it (9:7–10).

   Solomon doesn't want us to be morbid, discouraged, and oppressed in light of the certainty of death. He wants us to ask, "What does the approach of death mean to me *now*?" The answer comes when we embrace the reality of death and focus on the life we have to live before it arrives.

Verses 7–10 give us a recipe for joyful living:

a. Eat every meal like you're at a banquet (verse 7).

   Solomon wrote in Proverbs about coming to our meals with a glad heart (see Proverbs 15:17). Meals are to be occasions for celebration and fellowship, but far too often we eat on the run or while watching television. And it's not the food that's the issue; it doesn't have to be an expensive meal. It's what you bring to the table in your heart that matters.

   The modern concept of "fast food" goes contrary to Solomon's notion. In fact, there is a growing movement among food experts and connoisseurs called "Slow Food" which promotes a return to the Mediterranean and near Eastern ideas of meals as an extended event of socializing and fellowship—as well as the pure enjoyment of good food. This is certainly an extension of an ancient idea found in the Bible.

   Every meal that goes by without using it as an opportunity to interact with friends or loved ones is an opportunity missed.

b. Celebrate every day like you're at a party (verse 8).

   Putting on white garments and anointing one's head with oil were preparations for a party or celebration. Solomon is saying, "Do this every day—not just when there is a wedding or birthday or reunion. Make every day a celebration of life as a gift from God." The admonition to rejoice makes its way into the New Testament as well (Philippians 4:4; 1 Thessalonians 5:16). Even amidst a message of a world dying in sin, we find the admonition to always rejoice. Don't become preoccupied with death and forget that life is to be lived as a celebration of the goodness of God.

c. Enjoy every day of your marriage like you're on your honeymoon (verse 9).

   Remember that Solomon had violated his own marriage vows by importing wives from Egypt and having hundreds of concubines and wives in his harem. But there was a first wife, the wife of his youth, to whom he failed to stay faithful. It's important to note that, at the end of his life, he is admonishing his readers to "live joyfully with the wife whom you love." Lifelong marriage takes work and commitment, but it can be the source of unending joy when invested in daily.

d. Go to work every day like it was your last day to work (verse 10).

   I have read that if a person goes to work right out of college, by the time he reaches age 50, he will have worked 56,000 hours. How many of those hours, for the average Christian, have been lived for God? And what might be the impact if they were? That doesn't mean becoming a pastor or missionary. It means thanking God each day for the work you have to do and asking Him to use you in your job for His glory and honor.

Irish poet Evangeline Patterson made this observation that I think bears well on this point: "I was brought up in a Christian environment where because God had to be given preeminence, nothing else was allowed to be important. I have broken through to the position that because God exists, everything is important."

That viewpoint will allow us to see our work places as sacred—as places of worship and work blended together. Our work, in fact, becomes a form of worship as we do our work "heartily, as to the Lord and not to men" (Colossians 3:23).

These four admonitions from Solomon can transform our lives from ones of dullness and drudgery to ones of joy, anticipation, and expectation. They are reminiscent of a verse we have already covered in these lessons, Ecclesiastes 5:20: "For he will not dwell unduly on the days of his life, because God keeps him busy with the joy of his heart."

Do you dwell unduly on the days of your life? Do you worry about death and dying? God wants your attention in life to be focused on the joy of living, not on the certainty of dying. But not as a means of avoidance! If you know Christ, you are not afraid of death. You know that death is a doorway into His presence forever. And because you are so certain of that fact, you are free to focus on the life that is yours to live now—and to live it with joy!

The Complexity of Life (9:11–18)

In our pursuit of joy in this life, Solomon wants us to be realists. Life is not all sweetness and light. There will be harsh realities that can be upsetting if we are not aware of them and prepared for them.

In This Life, the Best Man Isn't Always Rewarded (9:11–12)

This is a well-known passage of Scripture that is worthy of duplicating here:

> I returned and saw under the sun that—
> The race *is* not to the swift,
> Nor the battle to the strong,
> Nor bread to the wise,
> Nor riches to men of understanding,
> Nor favor to men of skill;
> But time and chance happen to them all.
> For man also does not know his time:
> Like fish taken in a cruel net,
> Like birds caught in a snare,
> So the sons of men *are* snared in an evil time,
> When it falls suddenly upon them.

Solomon is reemphasizing an earlier message: Life isn't fair, the best man doesn't always win, sometimes you do your best and come in last. These are hard lessons for us to learn, and ones we would do well to teach our children because it is simply how life is. Far too many adults have not learned these lessons and find themselves in despair when things don't go the way they expect.

Who was the biggest guy in the Bible? Goliath—but he was killed by a teenager with a sling. The wealthiest man? Solomon, but he ruined his life with poor choices. The fastest? Joab's brother, but he got run through with a spear. The handsomest? Absalom, but his beautiful hair got hung in a tree and he was killed. The strongest? Samson, but he was tricked by a woman and captured. The race doesn't always go to the strongest, fastest, most handsome, wealthiest, or biggest.

Pursue life with everything at your disposal, but be a realist. Sometimes the best person isn't always rewarded in this life.

In This Life, a Good Man Isn't Always Remembered (9:13–18)

Solomon tells a little story about a poor man who saved a city from destruction but who was then forgotten by everyone. The evil ruler who was going to destroy the city got more press and attention than the one who saved the city.

Have you ever done the right thing and then felt you were ignored or overlooked for your contribution? Those experiences are painful, to say the least. But they are consistent with life in this world: unfair, unpredictable, disappointing, and below expectations—sometimes. Life is not always that way, but it is frequent enough that we need to be realists and plan on it.

How to plan? Live every day focused on life, not death or disappointment. Life is a good gift from God who sees every good work and rewards us accordingly.

What—and who—are you focused on today?

APPLICATION

1. Read 1 Corinthians 15:12–58.

   a. What were some of the people in Corinth saying about death and resurrection? (verse 12)

   b. What did their argument imply about Christ Himself? (verse 13)

   c. What did their belief say about the whole Christian faith? (verse 14)

   d. What did it say about Paul and the apostles? (verse 15)

   e. And what did it say about their own faith in Christ? (verse 17)

   f. How would you relate verse 19 to the message of this lesson?

   g. How many of the human race will die? (verse 22)

   h. What is the last enemy that Christ will destroy? (verse 26)

   i. What reason does anyone have for fearing something that Christ is going to destroy?

j. How does the quote from Isaiah 22:13 in verse 32 compare to similar words Solomon has used in Ecclesiastes? How does Paul use them here?

k. What does corruption refer to in verse 42? How does this compare with Solomon's "realism" in Ecclesiastes?

l. What do "incorruption," "glory," "power," and "spiritual" convey about this fearful thing called "death"? (verses 42–43)

m. What does verse 50 say about the necessity for death?

n. What ultimately swallows up death? (verse 54)

o. Why is it possible to thank God in the face of death? (verse 57)

2. Read Hebrews 2:14–15.
   a. Why did Jesus become flesh and blood? (verse 14)

   b. Who holds the power of death at present? (verse 14)

   c. What can the fear of death do to people? (verse 15)

d. What will Christ do for any who live in the fear of death? (verse 15)

e. Where do you stand regarding "the fear of death"? In bondage, or released by Christ?

3. What do the following verses suggest about the need to focus on today instead of fearing death in the future?

   a. John 9:4

   b. 2 Corinthians 6:2

DID YOU KNOW?

Ecclesiastes 9:7–9 bears a striking resemblance to a passage from *The Gilgamesh Epic,* a Sumerian writing from around 2000 B.C., long before Solomon's time. "Make thou merry by day and by night. Of each day make thou a feast of rejoicing. Day and night dance thou and play! Let thy garments be sparkling fresh, thy head be washed; bathe thou in water. Pay heed to the little one that holds on to thy hand. Let thy spouse delight in thy bosom!" If the parallel is more than coincidental, it shows that wisdom literature migrated between cultures in Solomon's day and that he was widely read.

Fools Rush In

Ecclesiastes 10:1–20

In this lesson we learn how wisdom can prevent the effects of foolish mistakes and choices.

OUTLINE

If we do something really destructive, it's usually because we've tolerated smaller instances of foolish behavior. Asking God for wisdom daily can keep little "foolishnesses" from becoming big ones—whether in personal behavior, leadership, the work setting, or our words.

I. Foolishness in Little Things

II. Foolishness in Leadership
- A. The Ego-Driven Leader
- B. The Easy-Going Leader
- C. The Engineered Leader
- D. The Evil Leader

III. Foolishness in the Labor Pool

IV. Foolishness in Language
- A. An Untamed Tongue
- B. An Unkind Tongue
- C. An Unwise Tongue
- D. An Undisciplined Tongue
- E. An Unreasonable Tongue
- F. An Unfaithful Tongue

OVERVIEW

Solomon is the author of a large part of the wisdom literature of the Old Testament. And in this section of Ecclesiastes, he returns to the theme of wisdom versus foolishness. Ecclesiastes 10 is like a cross-section of the book of Proverbs. The teacher-king dispenses one wise saying, proverb-like, after another.

He is going to warn us about foolishness in four different areas of life: little things, leadership, the labor pool, and language.

FOOLISHNESS IN LITTLE THINGS (10:1–3)

Solomon begins with a rather distasteful picture: A fly falls into a bottle of perfume, dies, and spoils the whole thing. A delightful aroma turns into a foul odor. In the same way, a little bit of foolishness can destroy the image of one respected for wisdom and honor. The use of a tiny fly as the image has a reason. We can be ruined by something just as relatively small. We don't have to make a huge mistake to be brought down; it can be something small, but senseless and foolish.

The Bible is filled with suggestions that little things can ruin big things. A little leaven can leaven a whole lump of dough (1 Corinthians 5:6); a little fox can spoil a whole vineyard (Song of Solomon 2:15); and the small tongue can change the direction of large things (James 3:5). In Southern California we know all too well that a tiny spark can cause a mammoth wild fire with huge damage to property and life.

Often we'll hear someone complain about being in trouble for something they did: "It wasn't any big deal . . ." All it takes is a "little deal" to ruin an otherwise good life.

We've already seen Solomon's words in Ecclesiastes 9:18, "but one sinner destroys much good." One person in a large group can cause huge amounts of trouble. Whether it's one word, one act, one person, one careless moment. It's the little things that can be the most destructive. We ought to pray daily for God to protect us from becoming the "fly" in the ointment of our life or somebody else's.

Verse two is not a statement against left-handed people. It's a cultural reference to Solomon's day. The right hand was thought to be the place of power and the left hand a place of weakness. It's another way for Solomon to say that a moment of weakness, or foolishness, characterizes a fool. A good example is the children's fable called "The Emperor's New Clothes." Remember what happened? The emperor walked around naked because he believed the lies of two men who came to town telling him they would dress him in the world's finest robes. His vanity overruled his sensibility and he made a fool of himself. Foolishness in little things can ruin even an emperor's life.

Foolishness in Leadership (10:4–7, 16–19)

All who are in leadership positions (and everybody leads someone) should take these next verses to heart about foolishness in leadership. There are four kinds of leaders who make foolish mistakes.

The Ego-Driven Leader (10:4)

This leader abuses those under him because his ego is the most important thing in his life. Woodrow Wilson once wrote that every man who takes office in Washington either grows or swells. He said, "When I give a man an office, I watch him carefully to see whether or not he is swelling or growing." Solomon wrote in Proverbs of the danger of a ruler who lacks self-control (16:32; 25:28).

What should you do if you are under a leader who swells instead of grows, whose ego is more important than those he leads? Solomon says, "Do not leave your post; for conciliation pacifies great offenses" (verse 4). Don't panic, don't quit your job, don't leave your post. Be biblical in your responses (Proverbs 15:1; 16:14; 25:15).

The Easy-Going Leader (10:5–7)

The opposite to the ego-driven leader is the easy-going leader who, often out of insecurity, fails to lead with appropriate strength. Desiring not to offend, he puts people in leadership who shouldn't be there. So the wrong people are leading and the right people are not (verse 7).

The Engineered Leader (10:16–17)

Sometimes people are put into leadership positions not because they're good leaders but for political reasons. Their appointments are arranged, not earned. They end up partying instead of leading. Solomon says beware of such childish, foolish leaders as these. They will enrich themselves at the expense of those they are supposed to lead.

The Evil Leader (10:18–19)

The evil leader is lazy—no questions asked. The organization is falling down around him because he is too lazy to lead. Because of his laziness, the kingdom he is leading is destroyed. Solomon addresses laziness thoroughly in Proverbs, and the evil leader is an example of laziness in leadership.

Foolishness in the Labor Pool (10:8–10)

In this section, Solomon points out things that can happen when foolishness reigns in the workplace. He gives us five examples:

1. A man digging a pit can fall into it and get hurt. A mortician friend of mine said something like this happened at a funeral. As the pallbearers approached the grave, carrying the casket, one of them tripped and fell into the grave.
2. A man tearing down a wall reaches his hand through and is bitten by a snake. Snakes love to hide in the cool, dark recesses of stone walls. But it's not smart to reach before looking.
3. A man in a stone quarry gets hurt by a large stone. That could hurt big time depending on the size of the stone. (There were no hard hats in Solomon's day.)
4. A man chopping wood is injured by a flying piece of wood. Or maybe the ax bounces off the log and cuts his leg. Who knows? Either way, the man is injured.
5. A man cuts wood with a dull ax and has to work twice as hard. If he would just invest time in sharpening the ax, he could save lots of time in the long run. He should work smarter instead of harder.

We probably have tools of our trade that need sharpening. We could work smarter instead of harder. And all of us could exercise more wisdom in the workplace.

Foolishness in Language (10:11–14)

Nowhere is the evidence of foolishness more apparent than in human speech. All of us have said things devoid of wisdom, things we wish we could reach out and grab and take back immediately after we uttered them. So Solomon next addresses foolishness in language. There are six ways our tongue can reveal our foolishness.

An Untamed Tongue (10:11)

In the days when snake charmers were common, Solomon uses a reference that is a little unfamiliar to us today. Snake charmers would use the swaying motion of a flute to "charm" and seemingly immobilize a snake. But Solomon warns that the snake can strike before the charmer even begins his work.

The tongue is no different. It can strike while you're getting ready to keep it under control. Just when you think you're the master of your tongue, it can make you look foolish. There is a time to speak and a time to remain silent, Solomon said in chapter three; but the tongue seems to have its own mind at times. And the more we babble, the more chance we have of looking foolish.

An Unkind Tongue (10:12)

A wise man's words will be gracious, but a foolish man's words will destroy others and eventually destroy him as well (Proverbs 10:32; 13:3; 21:23). Is there anything more destructive than the tongue? In his letter to the church, the apostle James says we can bridle a horse and steer a ship; but no one can control the tongue. You and I have both walked away from situations wondering how we could have said what we said. We would do anything to take it back, but we can't.

An Unwise Tongue (10:13)

This is the person who talks just for the sake of talking. Either they love to hear themselves talk, or they are insecure with silence. Their words are a stream-of-consciousness tape that plays non-stop as long as they're awake. This person sees no difference between words—they're all the same: Important! The trouble is, no one that he's around thinks so. He is foolish because of not knowing how to speak only when there is something meaningful to say.

An Undisciplined Tongue (10:14a)

A fool is full of words but does not realize he is saying nothing. Solomon warned against the undisciplined tongue in Proverbs: "In the multitude of words sin is not lacking, but he who restrains his lips is wise" (10:19). Roxanne Lulofs labels an undisciplined talker HARM—"Hit and Run Mouth." They will talk to anyone about anything, listening to no one. Dominance is the game, and attention is the goal.

Here's the epitaph of a former HARM:

"Beneath this stone, a lump of clay,
Lies Arrabella Young,
Who on the 24th of May
Began to hold her tongue."

It takes death to quiet the tongues of some.

An Unreasonable Tongue (10:14b–15)

The message of verses 14b–15 is summarized by Proverbs 27:1. "Do not boast about tomorrow, for you do not know what a day may bring forth."

Solomon is talking about someone who is always boasting about the future. Our inability to know the future is a theme Solomon has touched on several times in Ecclesiastes: "For who can bring him to see what will happen after him?" (3:22); "Who can tell a man what will happen after him under the sun?" (6:12); "For he does not know what will happen; so who can tell him when it will occur?" (8:7)

Solomon pokes a bit of fun at the person with the unreasonable tongue: The person is always boasting about the future, but does not even know how to get back to the city (verse 15b)! This is an Old Testament kind of understated humor. Picture a person babbling on about his great plans for the future, all the while totally lost. How could he ever find the future if he can't find his way back home?

An Unfaithful Tongue (10:20)

The message here? Never say anything—anything!—in private that you wouldn't say in public. Chances are good that what you say will make its way to the ears of those about whom you were speaking. You've heard the expression, "A little bird told me"? Solomon says that's how things you say can go from being private to public—a little bird. Obviously, birds don't talk. How things we intended to be private become public is just as mystifying as the idea of a bird talking. Solomon gives fair warning: It will happen, so don't consider being unfaithful with your tongue.

This potpourri of wisdom from Solomon has great practical value if we will but take it to heart. We have to be careful in life about the little things. Little compromises can have devastating results. We have to be careful about leadership—becoming or appointing or working under leaders who are foolish for one reason or another. We have to be careful in our day-to-day work. There are so many small mistakes and foolish choices we can make which can cause great injury and harm to ourselves or others. Finally, we have to be careful about our speech. This warning is the most important of all because the tongue is so explosive. Of course, it is not the tongue that is explosive, it is the human heart to which it is connected that is so dangerously volatile. Thus Solomon's exhortation in Proverbs to "keep your heart with all diligence" (4:23).

How do we assimilate such a wealth of practical advice? The best way I know is to turn to James 1:5: "If any of you lacks wisdom, let him ask of God, who gives to all liberally and without reproach, and it will be given to him." There's your answer. Get up every day and ask God for wisdom; ask Him for skill to navigate the shallows and shoals of life so you don't do or say something foolish and hurt yourself or another person.

James 1:5 is not just a Bible verse! It is a lifeline from God to you. It is God's daily message to you. It is not just for those times when you face a major crisis in life. It can be, and should be, your daily prayer to God: "Lord, give me wisdom today. Give me skill to walk my path today. Help me not to do or say anything foolish. I am naturally foolish in my heart, Lord. I can't be wise without You! Thank You for promising to hear and answer this prayer."

If you want to live a life of wisdom . . . want to avoid foolish mistakes and choices . . . make James 1:5 your prayer on a daily basis.

APPLICATION

1. From Proverbs 15, what do you learn about the powers of the tongue?

   a. verse 1

   b. verse 2

   c. verse 4

   d. verse 7

   e. verse 14

   f. verse 23

   g. verse 26

   h. verse 28

   i. What is the biggest temptation of foolishness for your own tongue?

   j. What is the wisest and most consistent way you use your words?

2. How might leaders best rule? (Proverbs 8:1, 15)

   a. What does a lack of followers indicate? (Proverbs 14:28)

b. What will foolish appointees incur from their leader? (Proverbs 14:35)

c. What must a leader guard against in terms of speech? (Proverbs 16:10)

d. What is the foundation of a leader's "rule"? (Proverbs 16:12)

e. What kind of "employees" do "leaders" love? (Proverbs 16:13)

f. What is the best way to handle an angry leader? (Proverbs 16:14)

g. What does a leader have the power to do? (Proverbs 19:12)

h. What characterizes a leader with longevity? (Proverbs 20:28)

i. What should "employees" do to win their "employers'" favor? (Proverbs 22:29)

3. What will happen if you forsake foolishness? (Proverbs 9:6)

a. How does a fool use his powers of speech? (Proverbs 10:18)

b. What's a quick way to tell if you're counseling a fool—or not? (Proverbs 12:15)

c. How quickly does a fool learn from his mistakes? (Proverbs 14:16)

d. What do fools think of instruction? (Proverbs 15:5)

e. What is the difference between what wise men seek and what fools seek? (Proverbs 15:14)

f. What impact does a fool have on his parents? (Proverbs 17:21)

g. What is a fool always focused on? (Proverbs 17:24)

h. How can a fool make himself appear wise to some degree? (verse 17:28)

4. What aspects of wisdom (or foolishness) did you find most applicable from this lesson?

DID YOU KNOW?

There are many instances in Scripture of the prominence of the right hand over the left as the hand of blessing, power, or authority. In Genesis 48:12–20, Jacob purposely crossed his hands in order to use his right hand to bless one of Joseph's sons over the other. God's right hand is described as the hand of power that defeated the Egyptians at the Exodus (Exodus 15:6, 12). Jacob's son Benjamin (*binyamin,* son of my right hand) was the object of special affection from his father. The law came from God's right hand (Deuteronomy 33:2). And, of course, Christ is currently at the right hand of God in heaven (Acts 7:55).

BEFORE IT'S TOO LATE

Ecclesiastes 11:1–12:14

In this lesson we review Solomon's teachings about the nature and meaning of life.

OUTLINE

Bookstore shelves are filled with volumes about "life" and how to find meaning in it. Very few of them can boil down their observations as succinctly as Solomon. He concluded His survey of how to find meaning in life with two simple prescriptions: Fear God and keep His commands.

I. Life Is Uncertain: Embrace It
- A. Be Diversified in Your Investments
- B. Be Diligent in Your Involvement

II. Life Is Short: Enjoy It
- A. Experience Each Day Totally
- B. Enjoy Your Youth Thoroughly
- C. Express Your Faith Thoughtfully
- D. Embrace Your Aging Thankfully

III. Life Is Mysterious: Examine It
- A. Wisdom Comes Through Instruction
- B. Wisdom Comes Through Insight
- C. Wisdom Comes Through Inspiration

IV. Life Is Obedience: Express It

OVERVIEW

During World War II, the prisoners of the Sobibor concentration camp in Eastern Europe started an uprising against their Nazi captors. Of the 700 prisoners who took part in the escape, 300 made it to the edge of the nearby forest. Of those, less than 100 are known to have survived. Three teenage boys were among those who were able to hide in the dense woods. They hid and slept during the day and traveled at night, fueled by the hope of survival.

After four nights of wandering, the boys came to a clearing and saw the silhouette of buildings against the sky. As they approached joyfully, they discovered the buildings were those of the Sobibor concentration camp! They had spent four days traveling in a circle. They were right back where they started.

While one of the three boys ultimately survived to tell his story to the world, the picture of them wandering in a circle is a picture of Solomon in the book of Ecclesiastes. This book describes his round-trip experience with God. He begins the book by saying that all is vanity, and he ends the book by saying the same thing (12:8). We conclude our study of Ecclesiastes by looking at chapters 11 and 12 together since the two chapters cover one lengthy theme.

We stated earlier in this series of lessons that Ecclesiastes is Solomon's book of regrets. He looks back upon his life from the perspective of old age and regrets that he tried to live the latter part of his life without keeping God at the center. In that way, life is like wandering through the woods without a map, ending up where you began: frustrated and meaningless. Life without God, Solomon concludes, is vanity and striving after the wind.

In this lesson, we find Solomon resolving all the questions he has raised in the first ten chapters of the book. In the 12th chapter he reaches what he calls "the conclusion of the whole matter: Fear God and keep His commandments" (12:13). He presents us with a summary of four final principles by which we can find meaning and enjoyment in our brief sojourn through this temporary world.

LIFE IS UNCERTAIN: EMBRACE IT (11:1–6)

Solomon has taken great pains to communicate the uncertainty of life throughout this book. There is a temptation for many who are Christians to just sit back and relax in the face of life's uncertainties: Play it safe, don't rock the boat, bide your time. Solomon takes a proactive, not a passive, approach to life—but does so with wisdom.

Be Diversified in Your Investments (11:1–2)

Here is another well-known idiom that arises from Ecclesiastes: "Cast your bread upon the waters" (verse 1). In Solomon's day, merchants would load their ships with grain and other goods and send them out to trade with other peoples. They hoped the ships would return laden with goods more valuable than those with which they departed. That was casting their bread upon the water. The plural "waters" indicated the wisdom of not sending all your grain in one ship, in one direction. Rather, diversify your investments so that if one ship isn't successful, others might be.

Today we talk of diversifying our investments so that if some go down in value, others will go up. Life is uncertain—instead of burying your resources in fear, invest them in a diversified manner.

Be Diligent in Your Involvement (11:3–6)

Diversification should be coupled with diligence. Instead of being passive and fearful about life, be bold and be strong. Work hard and expect that God is with you. If you work hard, there is no guarantee you will be successful; but if you don't work hard, there *is* a guarantee you will be unsuccessful.

We don't know which way the wind will blow, where the rain will fall, or if it will be sunny or cloudy. If a tree falls, we don't know which direction it will fall, nor do we know how a child grows in its mother's womb. All of these are uncertainties about life. But we cannot let these uncertainties cripple us.

Don't you dare adopt the posture that some Christians have taken: "I know I'm going to heaven, so I'll just take it easy until that happens." The opposite should be true: Because you know you are going to heaven, you should live passionately in this life.

Life Is Short: Enjoy It (11:7–12:8)

We are not going to stay young all our lives. Age is an unstoppable reality, so live your life totally, thoroughly, thoughtfully, and thankfully.

Experience Each Day Totally (11:7–9)

I love the seventh verse: "Truly the light is sweet, and it is pleasant for the eyes to behold the sun." Never take for granted the privilege of living another day. Anyone who has lived with a life-threatening illness or experience knows the truth of that statement. We ought to greet every new day with a "Thank you, Lord!" to show our gratitude to God for the privilege of being alive.

I love living in southern California because I get to greet the sun most days of the year.

Enjoy Your Youth Thoroughly (11:9–10)

One of the major themes of Solomon's book is that we are to enjoy life. Here he says specifically to young people: "Rejoice, O young man, in your youth" (verse 9).

I'm amazed at how young people think. When they're 16, they want to be 18. When they're 18 they want to be 21. And when they're 21 they want to be 25. Somewhere along the way, they start wanting to go backward instead of forward. But for so many years they are anxious to leave the "confines" of youth.

But Solomon says that youth is a time to be treasured. This is a message for parents as much as for young people: Don't force your kids to grow up sooner than necessary. Let them enjoy the freedom and opportunities of youth, for they will be over all too soon. I can remember talking with our children when they were college age about how great high school was. High school isn't a business like college; it's a place to grow and experience and be taken care of. Granted, it's only for a season, and responsibilities come soon. But young people should enjoy their youth and not long to be free of it.

Youth is not a time to sow wild oats—that's not Solomon's message. Instead, youth is a gift from God, just as adulthood is. The point is this: Don't be anxious to leave God's appointed times and seasons in your life, especially youth. Live them and enjoy them for all they're worth. *The Message* renders verse 10 this way:

"Live footloose and fancy free—
You won't be young forever.
Youth lasts about as long as smoke."

Because youth is fleeting, I encourage parents to let their kids be kids. I've seen too many adults who never got to be children, who try to recover their childhood once they're married. It's a recipe for disaster because, let's face it, kids do wild and crazy things. If young people were allowed to get some of those things out of their system when they're supposed to, they'd feel less need to do it as adults.

Express Your Faith Thoughtfully (12:1–2)

Twice in this last chapter Solomon admonishes his readers to remember their Creator in the days of their youth. Most people do the opposite: They put God on a shelf during the days of their youth saying, "I'll get serious about God when I'm a bit older."

If a strong foundation with God is laid during one's youth, it will be the basis for a lifetime of faith. "Remember" doesn't mean just a mental image, but a full commitment that involves heart, soul, mind, and strength. Learn spiritual disciplines and be spiritually accountable. Many adult Christians today (including myself) shudder to think where they might have ended up had they not laid a spiritual foundation in their lives when they were young.

Embrace Your Aging Thankfully (12:3–7)

For those of us who are no longer young, Solomon says we are to embrace our age thankfully. He paints a poetic picture of the signs of growing old which become motivation for living every day to its fullest while we're able.

- Verse 3: The "keepers of the house" are your arms and hands that tremble in old age. The "strong men" are your legs, knees, and shoulders that "bow down" and cause you to walk with a stoop. The "grinders . . . are few" means that we lose our teeth. "The windows grow dim" means that our eyesight fails.
- Verse 4: "The doors are shut" refers to our loss of hearing, while "grinders" again refers to teeth. If you "[rise] up at the sound of a bird" it means you get up at 4:00 A.M. with the birds like many old people do. The "daughters of music" refers to our voice beginning to quiver and weaken.
- Verse 5: To be "afraid of height" means just what it says, and "the almond tree blossoms" refers to our hair turning white. "The grasshopper is a burden" likens us to grasshoppers at the end of the summer when their life span is nearly over. If "desire fails," it means our libido decreases in old age. And "mourners" going about in the street refers, obviously, to our funeral procession.

Verse 6 contains several metaphors for death: loosening the silver cord, the golden bowl being broken, the pitcher being shattered, and the wheel being broken at the well. At death, "the dust will return to the earth as it was, and the spirit will return to God who gave it" (verse 7).

The point is, life is on a timetable. We know old age and death are coming, so enjoy your life while you can.

Did you hear the story of the octogenarian who wanted to play golf, but his vision was so bad he couldn't see where the ball landed? He got another 80-year-old who had perfect vision to play with him. So the first man hit his tee shot, and the second said, "I see just where your ball landed." But by the time they walked to where the ball was supposed to be, the second man couldn't remember where it was!

That's the way it is. If it's not our vision, it's our memory—or something else. Enjoy them all while you can!

Life Is Mysterious: Examine It (12:9–12)

In school, we study first and then take the exam. But in life, Solomon says, we get the exam and then we study.

Wisdom Comes Through Instruction (12:9)

Verse 9: "And moreover, because the Preacher was wise, he still taught the people knowledge; yes, he pondered and sought out and set in order many proverbs."

Wisdom Comes Through Insight (12:10)

Solomon, like Jesus Christ, taught words of truth: "The Preacher sought to find acceptable words; and what was written was upright—words of truth."

Wisdom Comes Through Inspiration (12:11–12)

Students love these two verses: "The words of scholars are like well-driven nails. . . . Of making many books there is no end, and much study is wearisome to the flesh."

Did you notice that "Shepherd" in verse 11 is capitalized? That is a reference, of course, to God who is the source of all wisdom. He is the one who drives wisdom home to our hearts "like well-driven nails." I have heard preachers interpret this admonition concerning books to mean that the Bible is the only book you should read. That is obviously incorrect. Where would we be without the many godly authors who help us understand better what the Bible says?

However, some people amass huge libraries of intellectual and philosophical books because they are into searching, not finding; questions, not answers. But God has ended the search and provided the answer in Jesus Christ who is "the way, the truth, and the life" (John 14:6). Let your study of books be about understanding the answer, not reveling in the search for truth.

Life Is Obedience: Express It (12:13–14)

Finally, we arrive at Solomon's ultimate conclusion—where he has been headed since the first verse. His "conclusion of the whole matter" is worth reproducing word for word:

"Fear God and keep His commandments,
For this is man's all.
For God will bring every work into judgment,
Including every secret thing,
Whether good or evil."

Fearing God means to honor and reverence Him and "keep His commandments." That is the bottom line for how to find meaning in life. It's like the song we sing in church sometimes,

"Trust and obey,
For there's no other way,
To be happy in Jesus,
But to trust and obey."
—John H. Sammis

I hope you will find meaning in life by Solomon's simple formula of fearing God and keeping His commandments—for there's no other way.

APPLICATION

1. What word characterized the way the children of Israel left Egypt? (Exodus 14:8; Numbers 33:3)

   a. Who makes the righteous bold? (Psalm 138:3)

   b. Compare who is bold in Proverbs 28:1 with who is bold in 1 Peter 5:8. What are the implications of this even match-up?

   c. Compare Peter and John's natural state with their state as Spirit-filled preachers. What did the Spirit make them? Acts 4:13

   d. What did the apostles pray for in Acts 4:29?

   e. How was their prayer answered? (Acts 4:31)

   f. What do you gather from the phrase "grew bold" in Acts 13:46?

   g. What should characterize our access and approach to God? (Ephesians 3:12; Hebrews 4:16)

   h. Why is it necessary to pray for boldness? (Ephesians 6:19–20; note the context)

   i. In the Old Testament, the High Priest entered fearfully into the Holy of Holies. Why are we now told to enter boldly? (Hebrews 10:19)

   j. What is the opposite of boldness . . . diligence . . . confidence?

   k. By which are you most characterized—boldness or its opposite?

   l. How does the Christian balance boldness, risk-taking, and humility?

2. Read Psalm 92:12–14.

   a. What signs of energetic, fruitful living do you find in verses 12–13?

b. How does this lifestyle change when they get older? (verse 14)

c. What signs of energy, enjoyment, and fruitfulness would an observer note in your life?

d. As you get older, what are you doing to keep from "getting into a rut"?

e. What new experiences have you had in the last six months that involove sharing your faith?

f. What plans do you have in the next six months that will add new dimensions to your enjoyment of life?

g. Who are you mentoring in the philosophy of enjoying life as a gift from God?

3. What are the most significant new lessons you will take away from this study of Ecclesiastes?

   a. How has Ecclesiastes corrected your life in some way?

   b. What new dimensions of God's character have you discovered?

DID YOU KNOW?

Jesus Christ's subtle use of the Old Testament is revealed to the careful reader. For instance, Ecclesiastes 11:5 may well form the backdrop for John 3:8. Nicodemus was "the teacher of Israel" and would undoubtedly have made the connection between Jesus' words and Ecclesiastes. Both passages deal with mysteries; Ecclesiastes deals with the unpredictable nature of the wind, while Jesus uses that unpredictability to illustrate the Spirit's work (wind and spirit are the same word in Hebrew [*ruach*]); Ecclesiastes refers to the body being formed in the mother's womb and Nicodemus asks if that is what is meant by "born again." The more of the Old Testament the Christian knows, the more full his reading of the New Testament will be.

ADDITIONAL BOOKS
BY DR. DAVID JEREMIAH

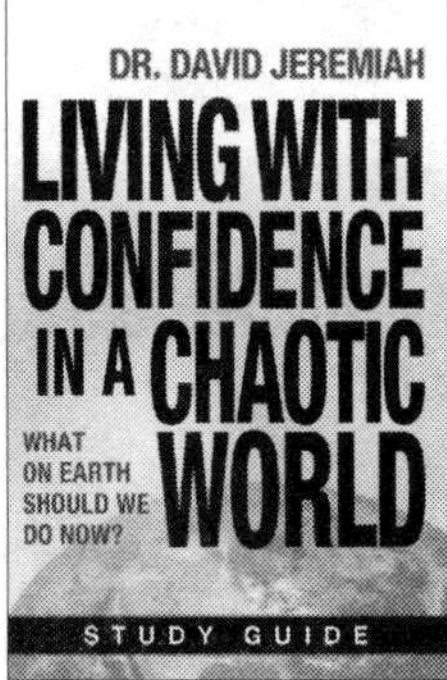

Living With Confidence in a Chaotic World

There is no doubt that our world is full of chaos and conflict. In *Living With Confidence in a Chaotic World,* Dr. David Jeremiah outlines ten biblical principles, each based squarely on the truth of God's Word, to provide a roadmap for living during these chaotic times.

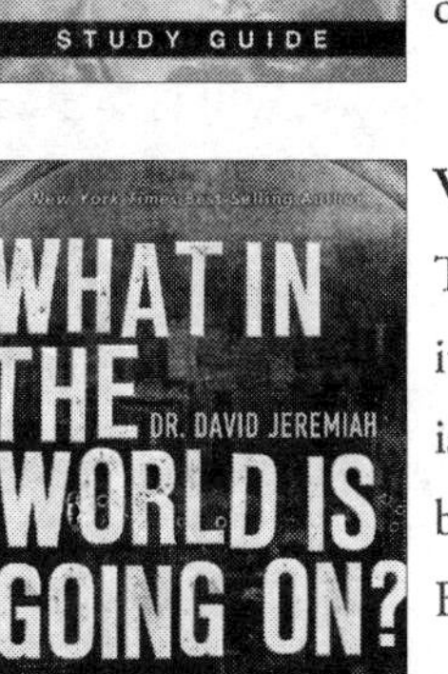

What in the World Is Going On?

The Bible has much to say about the End Times, yet it is hard to piece together all the information. That is why Dr. David Jeremiah has written a unique book that identifies the ten most essential clues to Bible prophecy.

Captured by Grace

Encountering grace changes lives forever. Let Dr. David Jeremiah show you how the transforming mercy that captured songwriter John Newton and the apostle Paul can awaken within you a fresh experience of the God who loves you fearlessly and pursues you with abandon.